Title: Al-Arba'īn An-Nawawīyah
Author: Abū Zakariyyā Yaḥyā Bin Sh
Edition: 1st
Published: 15th Ṣafar 1442H – 2nd Octc
Pages: 49
Editor: Abū Muḥammad 'Abd Allāh
Publisher: Takhrīj Al-Ḥadīth Publications
ISBN: 9 798687 699921
ASIN: B08KFYXGZN
Proofreader: 'Umm Muḥammad
Approved by: Shaykh Dr. 'Ādil Ḥasan Al-Ḥamad [1]
Shaykh Dr. Meḥbūb Abū 'Āṣim [2]
Shaykh Nazīr Aḥmad Madanī 'Umrī [3]

---

[1] https://twitter.com/adel_alhamad
[2] https://www.youtube.com/shaikhmehboobabuasim
[3] https://www.youtube.com/channel/UCTTZ1kiI76aGexC1qbF0ecQ

info@takhrijalhadith.com
https://takhrijalhadith.com
facebook.com/abumuhammadbh
patreon.com/takhrijalhadith
twitter.com/abumuhammadbh
instagram.com/takhrijalhadith

تخريج الحديث

Index

Foreword

بِسْمِ ٱللَّهِ ٱلرَّحْمَٰنِ ٱلرَّحِيمِ

All praise and thanks be to Allāh alone, the One, the Almighty, and the All-Merciful. Blessings and peace be upon Prophet Muḥammad, the last of His Messengers and Prophets, and upon his family, his Companions and all those who follow in his footsteps until the end of time.

We ask Allāh to make this a source of benefit for us and our deceased family members, and accept this little effort in serving the ḥadīth of our beloved Messenger (peace and blessings of Allāh be upon him), and may He enable us to achieve this task with all sincerity.

Our Research Criteria:

- Research refers to the references added in the footnotes.
- Research has been limited to the six books of the aḥādīth[1], as for the aḥādīth narrated in other books, the sources have been limited to only the ones quoted by Imām Nawawī. The referencing to Riyāḍ Us Ṣāliḥīn has also been added wherever applicable.
- Transliteration of the Arabic words into the English language.
- The books along their publications have been mentioned at the end of the book to know which numbering has been used.

And all perfect praise be to Allāh, Lord of the worlds.

Abū Muḥammad ‘Abd Allāh, Baḥrāin
15th Ṣafar 1442H – 2nd October 2020

(1) Ṣaḥīḥ Al-Bukhārī, Ṣaḥīḥ Muslim, Sunan Abī Dāwūd, Sunan An-Nasā’ī, Sunan At-Tirmidhī, and Sunan Ibn Mājah

الأَرْبَعِينَ النَّوَوِيَّة

تخريج الحديث

١- عَنْ أَمِيرِ الْمُؤْمِنِينَ أَبِي حَفْصٍ عُمَرَ بْنِ الْخَطَّابِ رَضِيَ اللهُ عَنْهُ قَالَ: سَمِعْتُ رَسُولَ اللَّهِ صَلَّى اللَّهُ عَلَيْهِ وَسَلَّمَ يَقُولُ: "إنَّمَا الْأَعْمَالُ بِالنِّيَّاتِ وَإِنَّمَا لِكُلِّ امْرِئٍ مَا نَوَى فَمَنْ كَانَتْ هِجْرَتُهُ إلَى اللَّهِ وَرَسُولِهِ فَهِجْرَتُهُ إلَى اللَّهِ وَرَسُولِهِ وَمَنْ كَانَتْ هِجْرَتُهُ لِدُنْيَا يُصِيبُهَا أَوْ امْرَأَةٍ يَنْكِحُهَا فَهِجْرَتُهُ إلَى مَا هَاجَرَ إلَيْهِ."

رَوَاهُ إِمَامَا الْمُحَدِّثِيْنَ: أَبُوْ عَبْدِ اللهِ مُحَمَّدُ بنُ إِسْمَاعِيْلَ بْن إِبْرَاهِيْمَ بْن الْمُغِيْرَةِ بْن بَرْدِزْبَهْ الْبُخَارِيُّ، وَأَبُوْ الْحُسَيْنِ مُسْلِمُ بْنُ الْحَجَّاجِ بن مُسْلِمٍ الْقُشَيْرِيُّ النَّيْسَابُوْرِيُّ رَضِيَ الله عَنْهُمَا فِيْ صَحِيْحَيْهِمَا اللَّذَيْنِ هُمَا أَصَحُّ الْكُتُبِ الْمُصَنَّفَة.

1 - It is narrated on the authority of 'Amīr Al-Mu'minīn Abī Ḥafṣ 'Umar Bin Al-Khaṭṭāb (may Allāh be pleased with him) who said: I heard the Messenger of Allāh (peace and blessings of Allāh be upon him) say:

"Indeed, The deeds are considered by the intentions, and a person will get the reward according to his intention. So whoever emigrated for Allāh and His Messenger, his emigration will be for Allāh and His Messenger; and whoever emigrated for worldly benefits or for a woman to marry, his emigration would be for what he emigrated for."

Narrated by the two Imāms of the Scholars of ḥadīth, Abū 'Abd Allāh Muḥammad Bin Ismā'īl Bin Ibrāhīm Bin Al-Mughīrah Bin Bardizbah Al-Bukhārī [d. 256H] and Abū Al-Ḥusayn Muslim Bin Al-Ḥajjāj Bin Muslim Al-Qushayrī An-Naisābūrī [d. 261H] (may Allāh be pleased with them) in their two ṣaḥīḥs which are the soundest of compiled books.(2)

:) Ṣaḥīḥ Al-Bukhārī (1, 54, 2529, 3898, 5070, 6689 & 6953); Ṣaḥīḥ Muslim (1907); Sunan Abī Dāwūd (2201); Sunan An-Nasā'ī '5, 3437 [3467] & 3794 [3825]); Sunan At-Tirmidhī (1647); Sunan Ibn Mājah (EN [4227] – AR [4367]); and Riyāḍ Us Ṣāliḥīn (1)

٢- عَنْ عُمَرَ رَضِيَ اللهُ عَنْهُ أَيْضًا قَالَ: "بَيْنَمَا نَحْنُ جُلُوسٌ عِنْدَ رَسُولِ اللَّهِ صَلَّى اللَّهُ عَلَيْهِ وَسَلَّمَ ذَاتَ يَوْمٍ، إِذْ طَلَعَ عَلَيْنَا رَجُلٌ شَدِيدُ بَيَاضِ الثِّيَابِ، شَدِيدُ سَوَادِ الشَّعْرِ، لَا يُرَى عَلَيْهِ أَثَرُ السَّفَرِ، وَلَا يَعْرِفُهُ مِنَّا أَحَدٌ، حَتَّى جَلَسَ إِلَى النَّبِيِّ صَلَّى اللَّهُ عَلَيْهِ وَسَلَّمَ، فَأَسْنَدَ رُكْبَتَيْهِ إِلَى رُكْبَتَيْهِ، وَوَضَعَ كَفَّيْهِ عَلَى فَخِذَيْهِ. وَقَالَ: يَا مُحَمَّدُ أَخْبِرْنِي عَنْ الْإِسْلَامِ. فَقَالَ رَسُولُ اللَّهِ صَلَّى اللَّهُ عَلَيْهِ وَسَلَّمَ: الْإِسْلَامُ: أَنْ تَشْهَدَ أَنْ لَا إلَهَ إلَّا اللَّهُ وَأَنَّ مُحَمَّدًا رَسُولُ اللَّهِ، وَتُقِيمَ الصَّلَاةَ، وَتُؤْتِيَ الزَّكَاةَ، وَتَصُومَ رَمَضَانَ، وَتَحُجَّ الْبَيْتَ إنْ اسْتَطَعْت إلَيْهِ سَبِيلًا. قَالَ: صَدَقْت. فَعَجِبْنَا لَهُ يَسْأَلُهُ وَيُصَدِّقُهُ! قَالَ: فَأَخْبِرْنِي عَنْ الْإِيمَانِ. قَالَ: أَنْ تُؤْمِنَ بِاَللَّهِ وَمَلَائِكَتِهِ وَكُتُبِهِ وَرُسُلِهِ وَالْيَوْمِ الْآخِرِ، وَتُؤْمِنَ بِالْقَدَرِ خَيْرِهِ وَشَرِّهِ. قَالَ: صَدَقْت. قَالَ: فَأَخْبِرْنِي عَنْ الْإِحْسَانِ. قَالَ: أَنْ تَعْبُدَ اللَّهَ كَأَنَّك تَرَاهُ، فَإِنْ لَمْ تَكُنْ تَرَاهُ فَإِنَّهُ يَرَاك. قَالَ: فَأَخْبِرْنِي عَنْ السَّاعَةِ. قَالَ: مَا الْمَسْئُولُ عَنْهَا بِأَعْلَمَ مِنْ السَّائِلِ. قَالَ: فَأَخْبِرْنِي عَنْ أَمَارَاتِهَا؟ قَالَ: أَنْ تَلِدَ الْأَمَةُ رَبَّتَهَا، وَأَنْ تَرَى الْحُفَاةَ الْعُرَاةَ الْعَالَةَ رِعَاءَ الشَّاءِ يَتَطَاوَلُونَ فِي الْبُنْيَانِ. ثُمَّ انْطَلَقَ، فَلَبِثْتُ مَلِيًّا. ثُمَّ قَالَ: يَا عُمَرُ أَتَدْرِي مَنْ السَّائِلُ؟ قُلْتُ: اللَّهُ وَرَسُولُهُ أَعْلَمُ. قَالَ: فَإِنَّهُ جِبْرِيلُ أَتَاكُمْ يُعَلِّمُكُمْ دِينَكُمْ." [رَوَاهُ مُسْلِمٌ]

2 - ʻUmar (may Allāh be pleased with him) also said:

While we were one day sitting with the Messenger of Allāh (peace and blessings of Allāh be upon him) there appeared before us a man dressed in extremely white clothes and with extremely black hair. No traces of journey were visible on him, and none of us knew him. He sat down close by the Prophet (peace and blessings of Allāh be upon him) rested his knees against the knees of the Prophet (peace and blessings of Allāh be upon him) and placed his palms over his thighs. And he said: "O Muḥammad! Inform me about Islām." The Messenger of Allāh (peace and blessings of Allāh be upon him) replied: "Islām is that you should testify that there is no deity worthy of worship except Allāh and that Muḥammad is His Messenger (peace and blessings of Allāh be upon him), that you should perform Ṣalāh (ritual prayer), pay the Zakāh, fast during Ramaḍān, and perform Ḥajj (pilgrimage) to the House (the Ka`bah at Makkah), if you can find a way to it (or find the means for making the journey to it)." The man said: "You have spoken truthfully." We were surprised that he asked him and then said he was truthful. He said: "Then, Tell me about faith (ʻĪmān)." The Prophet (peace and blessings of Allāh be upon him) said: "Faith is to believe in Allāh, His Angels, His Books, His Messengers, the Last Day, and to believe in the Divine Decree (Qadar), both its good and its evil." The man said: "You have spoken truthfully. Tell me about excellence (Iḥsān)." The Prophet (peace and blessings of Allāh be upon him) said: "Excellence is to worship Allāh as if you see Him, but if you don't see Him, He certainly sees you." The man said: "Tell me about [the time of] the Hour." The Prophet (peace and blessings of Allāh be upon him) said: "The one asked does not know more than the one asking." The man said: "Tell me about its signs." The Prophet (peace and blessings of Allāh be upon him) said: "The servant girl will give birth to her mistress and you will see barefoot, naked, and destitute shepherds compete in constructing tall buildings. Then the man left and I remained." The Prophet (peace and blessings of Allāh be upon him) said to me: "O ʻUmar, do you know who the questioner was?" I said: "Allāh and His Messenger know best." The Prophet (peace and blessings of Allāh be upon him) said: "Verily, he was Jibrīl who came to teach you your religion." [Narrated by Muslim][3]

۞۞۞

---

3) **Ṣaḥīḥ Muslim (8); Sunan Abī Dāwūd (4695); Sunan An-Nasā'ī (4990 [4993]); Sunan At-Tirmidhī (2610); Sunan Ibn Mājah EN [63] – AR [66]); and Riyāḍ Us Ṣāliḥīn (60)**

٣ - عَنْ أَبِي عَبْدِ الرَّحْمَنِ عَبْدِ اللهِ بْنِ عُمَرَ بْنِ الْخَطَّابِ رَضِيَ اللَّهُ عَنْهُمَا قَالَ: سَمِعْتُ رَسُولَ اللهِ صَلَّى اللَّهُ عَلَيْهِ وَسَلَّمَ يَقُولُ: "بُنِيَ الْإِسْلَامُ عَلَى خَمْسٍ: شَهَادَةِ أَنْ لَا إِلَهَ إِلَّا اللهُ وَأَنَّ مُحَمَّدًا رَسُولُ اللهِ، وَإِقَامِ الصَّلَاةِ، وَإِيتَاءِ الزَّكَاةِ، وَحَجِّ الْبَيْتِ، وَصَوْمِ رَمَضَانَ." [رَوَاهُ الْبُخَارِيُّ وَمُسْلِمٌ]

3 - On the authority of Abī 'Abdur-Raḥmān 'Abd Allāh Bin 'Umar Bin Al-Khaṭṭāb (may Allāh be pleased with them both) who said:

I heard the Messenger of Allāh (peace and blessings of Allāh be upon him) say: "Islām has been built on five [pillars]: Testifying that there is no deity worthy of worship except Allāh and that Muḥammad is the Messenger of Allāh, establishing the Ṣalāh (prayer), paying the Zakāh (obligatory charity), making the Ḥajj (pilgrimage) to the House, and fasting in Ramaḍān." [Narrated by Bukhārī and Muslim](4)

✡✡✡

(4) Ṣaḥīḥ Al-Bukhārī (8 & 4513); Ṣaḥīḥ Muslim (16); Sunan An-Nasā'ī (5001); Sunan At-Tirmidhī (2609); and Riyāḍ Us Ṣāliḥīn (1075, 1206 & 1271)

٤ - عَنْ أَبِي عَبْدِ الرَّحْمَنِ عَبْدِ اللَّهِ بْنِ مَسْعُودٍ رَضِيَ اللَّهُ عَنْهُ قَالَ: حَدَّثَنَا رَسُولُ اللَّهِ صَلَّى اللَّهُ عَلَيْهِ وَسَلَّمَ: وَهُوَ الصَّادِقُ الْمَصْدُوقُ: "إِنَّ أَحَدَكُمْ يُجْمَعُ خَلْقُهُ فِي بَطْنِ أُمِّهِ أَرْبَعِينَ يَوْمًا نُطْفَةً، ثُمَّ يَكُونُ عَلَقَةً مِثْلَ ذَلِكَ، ثُمَّ يَكُونُ مُضْغَةً مِثْلَ ذَلِكَ، ثُمَّ يُرْسَلُ إِلَيْهِ الْمَلَكُ فَيَنْفُخُ فِيهِ الرُّوحَ، وَيُؤْمَرُ بِأَرْبَعِ كَلِمَاتٍ: بِكَتْبِ رِزْقِهِ، وَأَجَلِهِ، وَعَمَلِهِ، وَشَقِيٍّ أَمْ سَعِيدٍ؛ فَوَاللَّهِ الَّذِي لَا إِلَهَ غَيْرُهُ إِنَّ أَحَدَكُمْ لَيَعْمَلُ بِعَمَلِ أَهْلِ الْجَنَّةِ حَتَّى مَا يَكُونُ بَيْنَهُ وَبَيْنَهَا إِلَّا ذِرَاعٌ فَيَسْبِقُ عَلَيْهِ الْكِتَابُ فَيَعْمَلُ بِعَمَلِ أَهْلِ النَّارِ فَيَدْخُلُهَا. وَإِنَّ أَحَدَكُمْ لَيَعْمَلُ بِعَمَلِ أَهْلِ النَّارِ حَتَّى مَا يَكُونُ بَيْنَهُ وَبَيْنَهَا إِلَّا ذِرَاعٌ فَيَسْبِقُ عَلَيْهِ الْكِتَابُ فَيَعْمَلُ بِعَمَلِ أَهْلِ الْجَنَّةِ فَيَدْخُلُهَا." [رَوَاهُ الْبُخَارِيُّ وَمُسْلِمٌ]

4 - On the authority of Abī 'Abdur-Raḥmān 'Abd Allāh Bin Mas'ūd (may Allāh be pleased with him) who said:

The Messenger of Allāh (peace and blessings of Allāh be upon him), and he is the truthful, the believed, narrated to us: "Verily the creation of each one of you is brought together in his mother's womb for forty days in the form of a nutfah (a drop), then he becomes an 'alaqah (clot of blood) for the same period, then a muḍghah (morsel of flesh) for the same period, then there is sent to him the angel who blows his soul into him and is commanded with four matters: To write down his rizq (sustenance), his life span, his actions, and whether he will be happy or unhappy (i.e., whether or not he will enter Paradise). By the One, other than Whom there is no deity, verily one of you performs the actions of the people of Paradise until there is but an arm's length between him and it, and that which has been written overtakes him, and so he acts with the actions of the people of the Hellfire and thus enters it; and verily one of you performs the actions of the people of the Hellfire, until there is but an arm's length between him and it, and that which has been written overtakes him and so he acts with the actions of the people of Paradise and thus he enters it." [Narrated by Bukhārī and Muslim][5]

✿✿✿

---

(5) Ṣaḥīḥ Al-Bukhārī (3208, 3332, 6594 & 7454); Ṣaḥīḥ Muslim (2643 & 2645); Sunan Abī Dāwūd (4708); Sunan At-Tirmidhī (EN [2137] – AR [2284]); Sunan Ibn Mājah (EN [76] – AR [80]); and Riyāḍ Us Ṣāliḥīn (396)

٥ - عَنْ أُمِّ الْمُؤْمِنِينَ أُمِّ عَبْدِ اللَّهِ عَائِشَةَ رَضِيَ اللَّهُ عَنْهَا، قَالَتْ: قَالَ رَسُولُ اللَّهِ صَلَّى اللَّهُ عَلَيْهِ وَسَلَّمَ: "مَنْ أَحْدَثَ فِي أَمْرِنَا هَذَا مَا لَيْسَ مِنْهُ فَهُوَ رَدٌّ." [رَوَاهُ الْبُخَارِيُّ وَمُسْلِمٌ]

وَفِي رِوَايَةٍ لِمُسْلِمٍ: "مَنْ عَمِلَ عَمَلًا لَيْسَ عَلَيْهِ أَمْرُنَا فَهُوَ رَدٌّ."

5 - On the authority of the mother of the believers Umm 'Abd Allāh, 'Ā'ishah (may Allāh be pleased with her) who said:

The Messenger of Allāh (peace and blessings of Allāh be upon him) said: "He who innovates something in this matter of ours (i.e., Islām) that is not of it will have it rejected (by Allāh)." [Narrated by Bukhārī and Muslim][6]

And in another narration by Muslim[7]: "He who does an act which we have not commanded, will have it rejected (by Allāh)."

✪✪✪

---

(6) Ṣaḥīḥ Al-Bukhārī (2697); Ṣaḥīḥ Muslim (1718); Sunan Abī Dāwūd (4606); Sunan Ibn Mājah (14); and Riyāḍ Us Ṣāliḥīn (16 & 1647)

(7) Ṣaḥīḥ Muslim (1718); and Riyāḍ Us Ṣāliḥīn (1647)

٦ - عَنْ أَبِي عَبْدِ اللهِ النُّعْمَانِ بْنِ بَشِيرٍ رَضِيَ اللَّهُ عَنْهُمَا، قَالَ: سَمِعْت رَسُولَ اللهِ صَلَّى اللَّهُ عَلَيْهِ وَسَلَّمَ يَقُولُ: "إنَّ الْحَلَالَ بَيِّنٌ، وَإِنَّ الْحَرَامَ بَيِّنٌ، وَبَيْنَهُمَا أُمُورٌ مُشْتَبِهَاتٌ لَا يَعْلَمُهُنَّ كَثِيرٌ مِنْ النَّاسِ، فَمَنْ اتَّقَى الشُّبُهَاتِ فَقْد اسْتَبْرَأَ لِدِينِهِ وَعِرْضِهِ، وَمَنْ وَقَعَ فِي الشُّبُهَاتِ وَقَعَ فِي الْحَرَامِ، كَالرَّاعِي يَرْعَى حَوْلَ الْحِمَى يُوشِكُ أَنْ يَرْتَعَ فِيهِ، أَلَا وَإِنَّ لِكُلِّ مَلِكٍ حِمًى، أَلَا وَإِنَّ حِمَى اللَّهِ مَحَارِمُهُ، أَلَا وَإِنَّ فِي الْجَسَدِ مُضْغَةً إذَا صَلَحَتْ صَلَحَ الْجَسَدُ كُلُّهُ، وَإِذَا فَسَدَتْ فَسَدَ الْجَسَدُ كُلُّهُ، أَلَا وَهِيَ الْقَلْبُ." [رَوَاهُ الْبُخَارِيُّ وَمُسْلِمٌ]

6 - On the authority of Abī 'Abd Allāh An-Nu'mān Bin Bashīr (may Allāh be pleased with them both) who said:

I heard the Messenger of Allāh (peace and blessings of Allāh be upon him) say: "That which is ḥalāl (lawful) is clear and that which is ḥarām (unlawful) is clear, and between the two of them are doubtful matters about which many people do not know. Thus he who avoids doubtful matters clears himself in regard to his religion and his honor, but he who falls into doubtful matters [eventually] falls into that which is ḥarām (unlawful), like the shepherd who pastures around a sanctuary, all but grazing therein. Truly every king has a sanctuary, and truly Allāh's sanctuary is His prohibitions. Truly in the body there is a morsel of flesh, which, if it be sound, all the body is sound, and which, if it is diseased, all of [the body] is diseased. Truly, it is the heart." [Narrated by Bukhārī and Muslim][8]

✡✡✡

---

(8) Ṣaḥīḥ Al-Bukhārī (52 & 2051); Ṣaḥīḥ Muslim (1599); Sunan Abī Dāwūd (3329); Sunan An-Nasā'ī (4453 [4458] & 5710 [5713]); Sunan At-Tirmidhī (1205); Sunan Ibn Mājah (3984); and Riyāḍ Us Ṣāliḥīn (588)

٧ - عَنْ أَبِي رُقَيَّةَ تَمِيمِ بْنِ أَوْسٍ الدَّارِيِّ رَضِيَ اللهُ عَنْهُ أَنَّ النَّبِيَّ صَلَّى اللَّهُ عَلَيْهِ وَسَلَّمَ قَالَ: "الدِّينُ النَّصِيحَةُ." قُلْنَا: لِمَنْ؟ قَالَ: "لِلَّهِ، وَلِكِتَابِهِ، وَلِرَسُولِهِ، وَلأَئِمَّةِ الْمُسْلِمِينَ وَعَامَّتِهِمْ." [رَوَاهُ مُسْلِمٌ]

7 - On the authority of Abī Ruqayyah Tamīm Bin Aus Ad-Dārī (may Allāh be pleased with him) who said:

The Prophet (peace and blessings of Allāh be upon him) said: "The dīn (religion) is naṣīḥah (advice, sincerity)." We said: "To whom?" He (peace and blessings of Allāh be upon him) said: "To Allāh, His Book, His Messenger, and to the leaders of the Muslims and their common folk." [Narrated by Muslim][9]

۞۞۞

---

(9) Ṣaḥīḥ Muslim (55); Sunan Abī Dāwūd (4944); Sunan An-Nasā'ī (4197 [4202] & 4198 [4203]); and Riyāḍ Us Ṣāliḥīn (181)

٨ - عَنْ ابْنِ عُمَرَ رَضِيَ اللَّهُ عَنْهُمَا، أَنَّ رَسُولَ اللَّهِ صَلَّى اللَّهُ عَلَيْهِ وَسَلَّمَ قَالَ: "أُمِرْتُ أَنْ أُقَاتِلَ النَّاسَ حَتَّى يَشْهَدُوا أَنْ لَا إلَهَ إلَّا اللَّهُ وَأَنَّ مُحَمَّدًا رَسُولُ اللَّهِ، وَيُقِيمُوا الصَّلَاةَ، وَيُؤْتُوا الزَّكَاةَ؛ فَإِذَا فَعَلُوا ذَلِكَ عَصَمُوا مِنِّي دِمَاءَهُمْ وَأَمْوَالَهُمْ إلَّا بِحَقِّ الْإِسْلَامِ، وَحِسَابُهُمْ عَلَى اللَّهِ تَعَالَى." [رَوَاهُ الْبُخَارِيُّ وَمُسْلِمٌ]

8 - On the authority of Ibn 'Umar (may Allāh be pleased with them both) who said:

The Messenger of Allāh (peace and blessings of Allāh be upon him) said: "I have been ordered to fight against the people until they testify that there is none worthy of worship except Allāh and that Muḥammad is the Messenger of Allāh, and until they establish the Ṣalāh (prayer) and pay the Zakāh (obligatory charity). And if they do that then they will have gained protection from me for their lives and property, unless [they commit acts that are punishable] in Islām, and their reckoning will be with Allāh, the Exalted" [Narrated by Bukhārī and Muslim][10]

۞۞۞

10) Ṣaḥīḥ Al-Bukhārī (25); Ṣaḥīḥ Muslim (22); and Riyāḍ Us Ṣāliḥīn (390, 1076 & 1209)

٩ - عَنْ أَبِي هُرَيْرَةَ عَبْدِ الرَّحْمَنِ بْنِ صَخْرٍ رَضِيَ اللهُ عَنْهُ قَالَ: سَمِعْت رَسُولَ اللَّهِ صَلَّى اللَّهُ عَلَيْهِ وَسَلَّمَ يَقُولُ: "مَا نَهَيْتُكُمْ عَنْهُ فَاجْتَنِبُوهُ، وَمَا أَمَرْتُكُمْ بِهِ فَأْتُوا مِنْهُ مَا اسْتَطَعْتُمْ، فَإِنَّمَا أَهْلَكَ الَّذِينَ مِنْ قَبْلِكُمْ كَثْرَةُ مَسَائِلِهِمْ وَاخْتِلَافُهُمْ عَلَى أَنْبِيَائِهِمْ." [رَوَاهُ الْبُخَارِيُّ وَمُسْلِمٌ]

9 - On the authority of Abī Hurayrah 'Abdur-Raḥmān Bin Ṣakhr (may Allāh be pleased with him) who said:

I heard the Messenger of Allāh (peace and blessings of Allāh be upon him) say: "What I have forbidden for you, avoid. What I have ordered you [to do], do as much of it as you can. For verily, it was only the excessive questioning and their disagreeing with their Prophets that destroyed [the nations] who were before you." [Narrated by Bukhārī and Muslim][11]

---

(11) Ṣaḥīḥ Al-Bukhārī (7288); Ṣaḥīḥ Muslim (1337); Sunan At-Tirmidhī (2679); Sunan Ibn Mājah (1 & 2); and Riyāḍ Us Ṣāliḥ (156)

١٠ - عَنْ أَبِي هُرَيْرَةَ رَضِيَ اللهُ عَنْهُ قَالَ: قَالَ رَسُولُ اللهِ صَلَّى اللهُ عَلَيْهِ وَسَلَّمَ: "إنَّ اللهَ طَيِّبٌ لَا يَقْبَلُ إلَّا طَيِّبًا، وَإِنَّ اللهَ أَمَرَ الْمُؤْمِنِينَ بِمَا أَمَرَ بِهِ الْمُرْسَلِينَ فَقَالَ تَعَالَى: ﴿يَا أَيُّهَا الرُّسُلُ كُلُوا مِنْ الطَّيِّبَاتِ وَاعْمَلُوا صَالِحًا﴾ وَقَالَ تَعَالَى: ﴿يَا أَيُّهَا الَّذِينَ آمَنُوا كُلُوا مِنْ طَيِّبَاتِ مَا رَزَقْنَاكُمْ﴾ ثُمَّ ذَكَرَ الرَّجُلَ يُطِيلُ السَّفَرَ أَشْعَثَ أَغْبَرَ يَمُدُّ يَدَيْهِ إلَى السَّمَاءِ: يَا رَبِّ! يَا رَبِّ! وَمَطْعَمُهُ حَرَامٌ، وَمَشْرَبُهُ حَرَامٌ، وَمَلْبَسُهُ حَرَامٌ، وَغُذِّيَ بِالْحَرَامِ، فَأَنَّى يُسْتَجَابُ لَهُ؟" [رَوَاهُ مُسْلِمٌ]

10 - On the authority of Abī Hurayrah (may Allāh be pleased with him) who said:

The Messenger of Allāh (peace and blessings of Allāh be upon him) said: "Allāh the Almighty is pure and accepts only that which is pure. And verily Allāh has commanded the believers to do that which He has commanded the Messengers. So, the Almighty has said: ﴿O (you) Messengers! Eat of the Ṭayyibāt [all kinds of ḥalāl (lawful) foods], and perform righteous deeds﴾(12) and the Almighty has said: ﴿O you who believe! Eat of the lawful things that We have provided you﴾(13) Then he (peace and blessings of Allāh be upon him) mentioned [the case] of a man who, having journeyed far, is disheveled and dusty, and who spreads out his hands to the sky saying: "O Lord! O Lord!" while his food is ḥarām (unlawful), his drink is ḥarām, his clothing is ḥarām, and he has been nourished with ḥarām, so how can [his supplication] be answered?" [Narrated by Muslim](14)

۞۞۞

---

12) Al-Qur'ān: Chapter 23 (Al-Mu'minūn), Verse: 51
13) Al-Qur'ān: Chapter 2 (Al-Baqarah), Verse: 172
14) Ṣaḥīḥ Muslim (1015); Sunan At-Tirmidhī (2989); and Riyāḍ Us Ṣāliḥīn (1851)

١١ - عَنْ أَبِي مُحَمَّدٍ الْحَسَنِ بْنِ عَلِيِّ بْنِ أَبِي طَالِبٍ سِبْطِ رَسُولِ اللَّهِ صَلَّى اللَّهُ عَلَيْهِ وَسَلَّمَ وَرَيْحَانَتِهِ رَضِيَ اللَّهُ عَنْهُمَا، قَالَ: حَفِظْتُ مِنْ رَسُولِ اللَّهِ صَلَّى اللَّهُ عَلَيْهِ وَسَلَّمَ: "دَعْ مَا يَرِيبُكَ إلَى مَا لَا يَرِيبُكَ".

[رَوَاهُ التِّرْمِذِيُّ وَالنَّسَائِيّ] وَقَالَ التِّرْمِذِيُّ: حَدِيثٌ حَسَنٌ صَحِيحٌ.

11 - On the authority of Abī Muḥammad Al-Ḥasan Bin 'Alī Bin Abī Ṭālib (may Allāh be pleased with them both), the grandson of the Messenger of Allāh (peace and blessings of Allāh be upon him), and the one much loved by him, who said:

I memorized from the Messenger of Allāh (peace and blessings of Allāh be upon him): "Leave that which makes you doubt for that which does not make you doubt."

[Narrated by At-Tirmidhī and An-Nasā'ī] And Tirmidhī said: It is a ḥasan ṣaḥīḥ ḥadīth.(15)

✡✡✡

---

(15) Sunan At-Tirmidhī (2518); Sunan An-Nasā'ī (5711 [5714]); and Riyāḍ Us Ṣāliḥīn (55)

١٢ - عَنْ أَبِي هُرَيْرَةَ رَضِيَ اللهُ عَنْهُ قَالَ: قَالَ رَسُولُ اللَّهِ صَلَّى اللَّهُ عَلَيْهِ وَسَلَّمَ: "مِنْ حُسْنِ إسْلَامِ الْمَرْءِ تَرْكُهُ مَا لَا يَعْنِيهِ."

[حَدِيثٌ حَسَنٌ، رَوَاهُ التِّرْمِذِيُّ وَغَيْرُهُ هٰكَذَا]

12 - On the authority of Abī Hurayrah (may Allāh be pleased with him) who said:

The Messenger of Allāh (peace and blessings of Allāh be upon him) said: “Part of the perfection of one’s Islām is his leaving that which does not concern him.”

[A ḥasan ḥadīth which was narrated by At-Tirmidhī and others like this][16]

۞۞۞

---

16) Sunan At-Tirmidhī (2317); Sunan Ibn Mājah (3976); and Riyāḍ Us Ṣāliḥīn (67)

١٣ - عَنْ أَبِي حَمْزَةَ أَنَسِ بْنِ مَالِكٍ رَضِيَ اللهُ عَنْهُ خَادِمِ رَسُولِ اللَّهِ صَلَّى اللَّهُ عَلَيْهِ وَسَلَّمَ عَنْ النَّبِيِّ صَلَّى اللَّهُ عَلَيْهِ وَسَلَّمَ قَالَ: "لَا يُؤْمِنُ أَحَدُكُمْ حَتَّى يُحِبَّ لِأَخِيهِ مَا يُحِبُّ لِنَفْسِهِ." [رَوَاهُ الْبُخَارِيُّ وَمُسْلِمٌ]

13 - On the authority of Abī Ḥamzah Anas Bin Mālik (may Allāh be pleased with him) — the servant of the Messenger of Allāh (peace and blessings of Allāh be upon him) — that the Prophet (peace and blessings of Allāh be upon him) said:

“None of you [truly] believes until he loves for his brother that which he loves for himself.” [Narrated by Bukhārī and Muslim][17]

---

(17) Ṣaḥīḥ Al-Bukhārī (13); Ṣaḥīḥ Muslim (45); Sunan An-Nasā'ī (5016 [5019], 5017 [5020] & 5039 [5042]); Sunan At-Tirmidh (EN [2515] – AR [2705]); Sunan Ibn Mājah (EN [66] – AR [69]); and Riyāḍ Us Ṣāliḥīn (183 & 236)

١٤ - عَنْ ابْنِ مَسْعُودٍ رَضِيَ اللهُ عَنْهُ قَالَ: قَالَ رَسُولُ اللَّهِ صَلَّى اللَّهُ عَلَيْهِ وَسَلَّمَ: "لَا يَحِلُّ دَمُ امْرِئٍ مُسْلِمٍ إلَّا بِإِحْدَى ثَلَاثٍ: الثَّيِّبُ الزَّانِي، وَالنَّفْسُ بِالنَّفْسِ، وَالتَّارِكُ لِدِينِهِ الْمُفَارِقُ لِلْجَمَاعَةِ." [رَوَاهُ الْبُخَارِيُّ وَمُسْلِمٌ]

14 - On the authority of Ibn Mas'ūd (may Allāh be pleased with him) who said:

The Messenger of Allāh (peace and blessings of Allāh be upon him) said: "It is not permissible to spill the blood of a Muslim except in three [instances]: The married person who commits zinā' (adultery), a life for a life, and the one who forsakes his dīn (religion) and separates from the community." [Narrated by Bukhārī and Muslim][18]

۞۞۞

---

18) Ṣaḥīḥ Al-Bukhārī (6878); Ṣaḥīḥ Muslim (1676); Sunan Abī Dāwūd (4352); Sunan An-Nasā'ī (4016 [4021] & 4721 [4725]); Sunan At-Tirmidhī (1402); and Sunan Ibn Mājah (2534)

١٥ - عَنْ أَبِي هُرَيْرَةَ رَضِيَ اللهُ عَنْهُ أَنَّ رَسُولَ اللَّهِ صَلَّى اللَّهُ عَلَيْهِ وَسَلَّمَ قَالَ: "مَنْ كَانَ يُؤْمِنُ بِاللهِ وَالْيَوْمِ الْآخِرِ فَلْيَقُلْ خَيْرًا أَوْ لِيَصْمُتْ، وَمَنْ كَانَ يُؤْمِنُ بِاللهِ وَالْيَوْمِ الْآخِرِ فَلْيُكْرِمْ جَارَهُ، وَمَنْ كَانَ يُؤْمِنُ بِاللهِ وَالْيَوْمِ الْآخِرِ فَلْيُكْرِمْ ضَيْفَهُ." [رَوَاهُ الْبُخَارِيُّ وَمُسْلِمٌ]

15 - On the authority of Abī Hurayrah (may Allāh be pleased with him), that the Messenger of Allāh (peace and blessings of Allāh be upon him) said:

"Let him who believes in Allāh and in the Last Day speak good, or keep silent; and let him who believes in Allāh and in the Last Day honour his neighbor; and let him who believes in Allāh and in the Last Day honour his guest." [Narrated by Bukhārī and Muslim][19]

✡✡✡

---

(19) Ṣaḥīḥ Al-Bukhārī (5185, 5186, 6018, 6136, 6138 & 6475); Ṣaḥīḥ Muslim (47 & 1468); Sunan Abī Dāwūd (5154); Sunan At-Tirmidhī (EN [2500] – AR [2688]); Sunan Ibn Mājah (3971); and Riyāḍ Us Ṣāliḥīn (308, 314, 706 & 1511)

١٦ - عَنْ أَبِي هُرَيْرَةَ رَضِيَ اللهُ عَنْهُ أَنَّ رَجُلًا قَالَ لِلنَّبِيِّ صَلَّى اللَّهُ عَلَيْهِ وَسَلَّمَ أَوْصِنِي. قَالَ: "لَا تَغْضَبْ." فَرَدَّدَ مِرَارًا، قَالَ: "لَا تَغْضَبْ." [رَوَاهُ الْبُخَارِيُّ]

16 - On the authority of Abī Hurayrah (may Allāh be pleased with him):

A man said to the Prophet (peace and blessings of Allāh be upon him): “Counsel me,” so he (peace and blessings of Allāh be upon him) said: “Do not become angry.” The man repeated [his request for counsel] several times, and [each time] he (peace and blessings of Allāh be upon him) said: “Do not become angry.” [Narrated by Bukhārī][20]

۞۞۞

---

(20) Ṣaḥīḥ Al-Bukhārī (6116); and Sunan At-Tirmidhī (2020); and Riyāḍ Us Ṣāliḥīn (48 & 639)

١٧ - عَنْ أَبِي يَعْلَى شَدَّادِ بْنِ أَوْسٍ رَضِيَ اللهُ عَنْهُ عَنْ رَسُولِ اللَّهِ صَلَّى اللَّهُ عَلَيْهِ وَسَلَّمَ قَالَ: "إنَّ اللَّهَ كَتَبَ الْإِحْسَانَ عَلَى كُلِّ شَيْءٍ، فَإِذَا قَتَلْتُمْ فَأَحْسِنُوا الْقِتْلَةَ، وَإِذَا ذَبَحْتُمْ فَأَحْسِنُوا الذِّبْحَةَ، وَلْيُحِدَّ أَحَدُكُمْ شَفْرَتَهُ، وَلْيُرِحْ ذَبِيحَتَهُ." [رَوَاهُ مُسْلِمٌ]

17 - On the authority of Abī Ya'lā Shaddād Bin Aws (may Allāh be pleased with him), that the Messenger of Allāh (peace and blessings of Allāh be upon him) said:

"Verily Allāh has prescribed iḥsān (proficiency, perfection) in all things. So, if you kill then kill well; and if you slaughter, then slaughter well. Let each one of you sharpen his blade and let him spare suffering to the animal he slaughters." [Narrated by Muslim][21]

✡✡✡

---

(21) Ṣaḥīḥ Muslim (1955); Sunan Abī Dāwūd (2815); Sunan An-Nasā'ī (4405 [4410], 4411 [4416], 4412 [4417], 4413 [4418] 4414 [4419]); Sunan At-Tirmidhī (1409); Sunan Ibn Mājah (EN [3170] – AR [3290]); and Riyāḍ Us Ṣāliḥīn (640)

١٨ - عَنْ أَبِي ذَرٍّ جُنْدُبِ بْنِ جُنَادَةَ، وَأَبِي عَبْدِ الرَّحْمَنِ مُعَاذِ بْنِ جَبَلٍ رَضِيَ اللَّهُ عَنْهُمَا، عَنْ رَسُولِ اللَّهِ صَلَّى اللَّهُ عَلَيْهِ وَسَلَّمَ قَالَ: "اتَّقِ اللَّهَ حَيْثُمَا كُنْت، وَأَتْبِعِ السَّيِّئَةَ الْحَسَنَةَ تَمْحُهَا، وَخَالِقْ النَّاسَ بِخُلُقٍ حَسَنٍ."

[رَوَاهُ التِّرْمِذِيُّ وَقَالَ: حَدِيثٌ حَسَنٌ، وَفِي بَعْضِ النُّسَخِ: حَسَنٌ صَحِيحٌ]

18 - On the authority of Abī Dharr Jundub Bin Junādah, and Abī 'Abdur-Raḥmān Mu'ādh Bin Jabal (may Allāh be pleased with them both), that the Messenger of Allāh (peace and blessings of Allāh be upon him) said:

"Have taqwā (fear) of Allāh wherever you may be, and follow up a bad deed with a good deed which will wipe it out, and behave well towards the people."

[It was narrated by At-Tirmidhī, who said it was a ḥasan ḥadīth, and in some copies, it is stated to be a ḥasan ṣaḥīḥ ḥadīth][22]

---

22) Sunan At-Tirmidhī (1987); and Riyāḍ Us Ṣāliḥīn (61)

١٩ - عَنْ أَبِي العَبَّاسِ عَبْدِ اللَّهِ بْنِ عَبَّاسٍ رَضِيَ اللَّهُ عَنْهُمَا قَالَ: "كُنْتُ خَلْفَ رَسُولِ اللَّهِ صَلَّى اللَّهُ عَلَيْهِ وَسَلَّمَ يَوْمًا، فَقَالَ: يَا غُلَامُ! إِنِّي أُعَلِّمُكَ كَلِمَاتٍ: احْفَظِ اللَّهَ يَحْفَظْكَ، احْفَظِ اللَّهَ تَجِدْهُ تُجَاهَكَ، إِذَا سَأَلْتَ فَاسْأَلِ اللَّهَ، وَإِذَا اسْتَعَنْتَ فَاسْتَعِنْ بِاللَّهِ، وَاعْلَمْ أَنَّ الْأُمَّةَ لَوِ اجْتَمَعَتْ عَلَى أَنْ يَنْفَعُوكَ بِشَيْءٍ لَمْ يَنْفَعُوكَ إِلَّا بِشَيْءٍ قَدْ كَتَبَهُ اللَّهُ لَكَ، وَإِنِ اجْتَمَعُوا عَلَى أَنْ يَضُرُّوكَ بِشَيْءٍ لَمْ يَضُرُّوكَ إِلَّا بِشَيْءٍ قَدْ كَتَبَهُ اللَّهُ عَلَيْكَ؛ رُفِعَتِ الْأَقْلَامُ، وَجَفَّتِ الصُّحُفُ."

[رَوَاهُ التِّرْمِذِيُّ – وَقَالَ: حَدِيثٌ حَسَنٌ صَحِيحٌ]

وَفِي رِوَايَةٍ غَيْرِ التِّرْمِذِيِّ: "احْفَظِ اللَّهَ تَجِدْهُ أَمَامَكَ، تَعَرَّفْ إِلَى اللَّهِ فِي الرَّخَاءِ يَعْرِفْكَ فِي الشِّدَّةِ، وَاعْلَمْ أَنَّ مَا أَخْطَأَكَ لَمْ يَكُنْ لِيُصِيبَكَ، وَمَا أَصَابَكَ لَمْ يَكُنْ لِيُخْطِئَكَ، وَاعْلَمْ أَنَّ النَّصْرَ مَعَ الصَّبْرِ، وَأَنَّ الْفَرَجَ مَعَ الْكَرْبِ، وَأَنَّ مَعَ الْعُسْرِ يُسْرًا."

19 - On the authority of Abī 'Abbās 'Abd Allāh Bin 'Abbās (may Allāh be pleased with them both) who said:

One day I was behind the Prophet (peace and blessings of Allāh be upon him) [riding on the same mount] and he said: "O young man, I shall teach you some words [of advice]: Be mindful of Allāh and Allāh will protect you. Be mindful of Allāh and you will find Him in front of you. If you ask, then ask Allāh [alone]; and if you seek help, then seek help from Allāh [alone]. And know that if the nation were to gather together to benefit you with anything, they would not benefit you except with what Allāh had already prescribed for you. And if they were to gather together to harm you with anything, they would not harm you except with what Allāh had already prescribed against you. The pens have been lifted and the pages have dried."

[It was narrated by At-Tirmidhī, who said it is a ḥasan ṣaḥīḥ ḥadīth][23]

Another narration, other than that of At-Tirmidhī: "Be mindful of Allāh, and you will find Him in front of you. Recognize and acknowledge Allāh in times of ease and prosperity, and He will remember you in times of adversity. And know that what has passed you by [and you have failed to attain] was not going to befall you, and what has befallen you was not going to pass you by. And know that victory comes with patience, relief with affliction, and hardship with ease."[24]

---

(23) Sunan At-Tirmidhī (EN [2516] – AR [2706]); and Riyāḍ Us Ṣāliḥīn (62)
(24) Musnad Aḥmad (Ḥadīth no. 2803 (pg. 18-21, vol 5)); and Riyāḍ Us Ṣāliḥīn (62)

٢٠ - عَنْ أَبِي مَسْعُودٍ عُقْبَةَ بْنِ عَمْرٍو الْأَنْصَارِيِّ الْبَدْرِيِّ رَضِيَ اللهُ عَنْهُ قَالَ: قَالَ رَسُولُ اللهِ صَلَّى اللهُ عَلَيْهِ وَسَلَّمَ: "إنَّ مِمَّا أَدْرَكَ النَّاسُ مِنْ كَلَامِ النُّبُوَّةِ الْأُولَى: إذَا لَمْ تَسْتَحِ فَاصْنَعْ مَا شِئْتَ." [رَوَاهُ الْبُخَارِيُّ]

20 - On the authority of Abī Mas'ūd 'Uqbah Bin 'Amr Al-Anṣārī Al-Badrī (may Allāh be pleased with him) who said:

The Messenger of Allāh (peace and blessings of Allāh be upon him) said: "Verily, from what was learnt by the people from the speech of the earliest prophecy is: If you feel no shame, then do as you wish." [Narrated by Bukhārī][25]

✡✡✡

---

(25) Ṣaḥīḥ Al-Bukhārī (3483, 3484 & 6120); Sunan Abī Dāwūd (4797); Sunan Ibn Mājah (4183); and Riyāḍ Us Ṣāliḥīn (1844)

٢١ - عَنْ أَبِي عَمْرٍو وَقِيلَ: أَبِي عَمْرَةَ سُفْيَانَ بْنِ عَبْدِ اللَّهِ رَضِيَ اللهُ عَنْهُ قَالَ: "قُلْت: يَا رَسُولَ اللَّهِ! قُلْ لِي فِي الْإِسْلَامِ قَوْلًا لَا أَسْأَلُ عَنْهُ أَحَدًا غَيْرَك." قَالَ: "قُلْ: آمَنْت بِاَللَّهِ ثُمَّ اسْتَقِمْ." [رَوَاهُ مُسْلِمٌ]

21 - On the authority of Abī `Amr and he is also called Abī `Amrah Sufyān Bin ‘Abd Allāh (may Allāh be pleased with him) who said:

I said: “O Messenger of Allāh, tell me something about Islām which I can ask of no one but you.” He (peace and blessings of Allāh be upon him) said: “Say I believe in Allāh and then be steadfast on it.” [Narrated by Muslim][26]

---

(26) Ṣaḥīḥ Muslim (38); Sunan At-Tirmidhī (2410); Sunan Ibn Mājah (3972); and Riyāḍ Us Ṣāliḥīn (85)

٢٢ - عَنْ أَبِي عَبْدِ اللَّهِ جَابِرِ بْنِ عَبْدِ اللَّهِ الْأَنْصَارِيِّ رَضِيَ اللَّهُ عَنْهُمَا: "أَنَّ رَجُلًا سَأَلَ رَسُولَ اللَّهِ صَلَّى اللَّهُ عَلَيْهِ وَسَلَّمَ فَقَالَ: أَرَأَيْت إذَا صَلَّيْت الْمَكْتُوبَاتِ، وَصُمْت رَمَضَانَ، وَأَحْلَلْت الْحَلَالَ، وَحَرَّمْت الْحَرَامَ، وَلَمْ أَزِدْ عَلَى ذَلِكَ شَيْئًا؛ أَأَدْخُلُ الْجَنَّةَ؟ قَالَ: نَعَمْ." [رَوَاهُ مُسْلِمٌ]

22 - On the authority of Abī 'Abd Allāh Jābīr Bin 'Abd Allāh Al-Anṣārī (may Allāh be pleased with them both) that:

A man questioned the Messenger of Allāh (peace and blessings of Allāh be upon him) and said: "Do you think that if I perform the obligatory prayers, fast in Ramaḍān, treat as lawful that which is ḥalāl, and treat as forbidden that which is ḥarām, and do not increase upon that [in voluntary good deeds], then I shall enter Paradise?" He (peace and blessings of Allāh be upon him) replied: "Yes." [Narrated by Muslim][27]

۞۞۞

(27) Ṣaḥīḥ Muslim (15)

٢٣ - عَنْ أَبِي مَالِكٍ الْحَارِثِ بْنِ عَاصِمٍ الْأَشْعَرِيِّ رَضِيَ اللهُ عَنْهُ قَالَ: قَالَ رَسُولُ اللَّهِ صَلَّى اللَّهُ عَلَيْهِ وَسَلَّمَ: "الطُّهُورُ شَطْرُ الْإِيمَانِ، وَالْحَمْدُ لِلَّهِ تَمْلَأُ الْمِيزَانَ، وَسُبْحَانَ اللهِ وَالْحَمْدُ لِلَّهِ تَمْلَآنِ - أَوْ: تَمْلَأُ - مَا بَيْنَ السَّمَاءِ وَالْأَرْضِ، وَالصَّلَاةُ نُورٌ، وَالصَّدَقَةُ بُرْهَانٌ، وَالصَّبْرُ ضِيَاءٌ، وَالْقُرْآنُ حُجَّةٌ لَك أَوْ عَلَيْك، كُلُّ النَّاسِ يَغْدُو، فَبَائِعٌ نَفْسَهُ فَمُعْتِقُهَا أَوْ مُوبِقُهَا." [رَوَاهُ مُسْلِمٌ]

23 - On the authority of Abī Mālik Al-Ḥārith Bin 'Āṣim Al-Ash'arī (may Allāh be pleased with him) who said:

The Messenger of Allāh (peace and blessings of Allāh be upon him) said: "Purity is half of 'Īmān (faith). Alḥamdulillāh (praise be to Allāh) fills the scales, and Subḥānallāh (how far is Allāh from every imperfection) and Alḥamdulillāh (praise be to Allāh) fills that which is between heaven and earth. And the Ṣalāh (prayer) is a light, and charity is a proof, and patience is illumination, and the Qur'ān is a proof either for you or against you. Every person starts his day as a vendor of his soul, either freeing it or causing its ruin." [Narrated by Muslim](28)

✡✡✡

---

(28) Ṣaḥīḥ Muslim (223); Sunan An-Nasā'ī (2437 [2439]); Sunan At-Tirmidhī (3517); Sunan Ibn Mājah (EN [280] – AR [293 and Riyāḍ Us Ṣāliḥīn (25, 1031 & 1413)

٢٤ - عَنْ أَبِي ذَرٍّ الْغِفَارِيِّ رَضِيَ اللهُ عَنْهُ عَنِ النَّبِيِّ صَلَّى اللهُ عَلَيْهِ وَسَلَّمَ فِيمَا يَرْوِيهِ عَنْ رَبِّهِ تَبَارَكَ وَتَعَالَى، أَنَّهُ قَالَ: "يَا عِبَادِي: إِنِّي حَرَّمْتُ الظُّلْمَ عَلَى نَفْسِي، وَجَعَلْتهُ بَيْنَكُمْ مُحَرَّمًا؛ فَلَا تَظَالَمُوا. يَا عِبَادِي! كُلُّكُمْ ضَالٌّ إِلَّا مَنْ هَدَيْتهُ، فَاسْتَهْدُونِي أَهْدِكُمْ. يَا عِبَادِي! كُلُّكُمْ جَائِعٌ إِلَّا مَنْ أَطْعَمْتهُ، فَاسْتَطْعِمُونِي أُطْعِمْكُمْ. يَا عِبَادِي! كُلُّكُمْ عَارٍ إِلَّا مَنْ كَسَوْتهُ، فَاسْتَكْسُونِي أَكْسُكُمْ. يَا عِبَادِي! إِنَّكُمْ تُخْطِئُونَ بِاللَّيْلِ وَالنَّهَارِ، وَأَنَا أَغْفِرُ الذُّنُوبَ جَمِيعًا؛ فَاسْتَغْفِرُونِي أَغْفِرْ لَكُمْ. يَا عِبَادِي! إِنَّكُمْ لَنْ تَبْلُغُوا ضَرِّي فَتَضُرُّونِي، وَلَنْ تَبْلُغُوا نَفْعِي فَتَنْفَعُونِي. يَا عِبَادِي! لَوْ أَنَّ أَوَّلَكُمْ وَآخِرَكُمْ وَإِنْسَكُمْ وَجِنَّكُمْ كَانُوا عَلَى أَتْقَى قَلْبِ رَجُلٍ وَاحِدٍ مِنْكُمْ، مَا زَادَ ذَلِكَ فِي مُلْكِي شَيْئًا. يَا عِبَادِي! لَوْ أَنَّ أَوَّلَكُمْ وَآخِرَكُمْ وَإِنْسَكُمْ وَجِنَّكُمْ كَانُوا عَلَى أَفْجَرِ قَلْبِ رَجُلٍ وَاحِدٍ مِنْكُمْ، مَا نَقَصَ ذَلِكَ مِنْ مُلْكِي شَيْئًا. يَا عِبَادِي! لَوْ أَنَّ أَوَّلَكُمْ وَآخِرَكُمْ وَإِنْسَكُمْ وَجِنَّكُمْ قَامُوا فِي صَعِيدٍ وَاحِدٍ، فَسَأَلُونِي، فَأَعْطَيْتُ كُلَّ وَاحِدٍ مَسْأَلَتَه، مَا نَقَصَ ذَلِكَ مِمَّا عِنْدِي إِلَّا كَمَا يَنْقُصُ الْمِخْيَطُ إِذَا أُدْخِلَ الْبَحْرَ. يَا عِبَادِي! إِنَّمَا هِيَ أَعْمَالُكُمْ أُحْصِيهَا لَكُمْ، ثُمَّ أُوَفِّيكُمْ إِيَّاهَا؛ فَمَنْ وَجَدَ خَيْرًا فَلْيَحْمَدِ اللهَ، وَمَنْ وَجَدَ غَيْرَ ذَلِكَ فَلَا يَلُومَنَّ إِلَّا نَفْسَهُ." [رَوَاهُ مُسْلِمٌ]

24 - On the authority of Abī Dharr Al-Ghifārī (may Allāh be pleased with him) from the Prophet (peace and blessings of Allāh be upon him) from his Lord (Glorified and Exalted be He), that He said:

"O My servants! I have forbidden Ẓulm (oppression) for Myself, and I have made it forbidden amongst you, so do not oppress one another. O My servants, all of you are astray except those whom I have guided, so seek guidance from Me and I shall guide you. O My servants, all of you are hungry except those whom I have fed, so seek food from Me and I shall feed you. O My servants; all of you are naked except those whom I have clothed, so seek clothing from Me and I shall clothe you. O My servants, you commit sins by day and by night, and I forgive all sins, so seek forgiveness from Me and I shall forgive you. O My servants, you will not attain harming Me so as to harm Me, and you will not attain benefiting Me so as to benefit Me. O My servants, if the first of you and the last of you, and the humans of you and the jinn of you, were all as pious as the most pious heart of any individual amongst you, then this would not increase My Kingdom an iota. O My servants, if the first of you and the last of you, and the humans of you and the jinn of you, were all as wicked as the most wicked heart of any individual amongst you, then this would not decrease My Kingdom an iota. O My servants, if the first of you and the last of you, and the humans of you and the jinn of you, were all to stand together in one place and ask of Me, and I were to give everyone what he requested, then that would not decrease what I Possess, except what is decreased of the ocean when a needle is dipped into it. O My servants, it is but your deeds that I account for you, and then recompense you for. So, he who finds good, let him praise Allāh, and he who finds other than that, let him blame no one but himself." [Narrated by Muslim][29]

[29] Ṣaḥīḥ Muslim (2577); Sunan At-Tirmidhī (EN [2495] – AR [2683]); Sunan Ibn Mājah (EN [4257] – AR [4398]); and Riyāḍ Us Ṣāliḥīn (111)

٢٥ - عَنْ أَبِي ذَرٍّ رَضِيَ اللهُ عَنْهُ أَيْضًا: "أَنَّ نَاسًا مِنْ أَصْحَابِ رَسُولِ اللهِ صَلَّى اللهُ عَلَيْهِ وَسَلَّمَ قَالُوا لِلنَّبِيِّ صَلَّى اللهُ عَلَيْهِ وَسَلَّمَ يَا رَسُولَ اللهِ ذَهَبَ أَهْلُ الدُّثُورِ بِالْأُجُورِ؛ يُصَلُّونَ كَمَا نُصَلِّي، وَيَصُومُونَ كَمَا نَصُومُ، وَيَتَصَدَّقُونَ بِفُضُولِ أَمْوَالِهِمْ. قَالَ: أَوَلَيْسَ قَدْ جَعَلَ اللهُ لَكُمْ مَا تَصَّدَّقُونَ؟ إنَّ بِكُلِّ تَسْبِيحَةٍ صَدَقَةً، وَكُلِّ تَكْبِيرَةٍ صَدَقَةً، وَكُلِّ تَحْمِيدَةٍ صَدَقَةً، وَكُلِّ تَهْلِيلَةٍ صَدَقَةً، وَأَمْرٌ بِالْمَعْرُوفِ صَدَقَةٌ، وَنَهْيٌ عَنْ مُنْكَرٍ صَدَقَةٌ، وَفِي بُضْعِ أَحَدِكُمْ صَدَقَةٌ. قَالُوا: يَا رَسُولَ اللهِ أَيَأْتِي أَحَدُنَا شَهْوَتَهُ وَيَكُونُ لَهُ فِيهَا أَجْرٌ؟ قَالَ: أَرَأَيْتُمْ لَوْ وَضَعَهَا فِي حَرَامٍ أَكَانَ عَلَيْهِ وِزْرٌ؟ فَكَذَلِكَ إذَا وَضَعَهَا فِي الْحَلَالِ، كَانَ لَهُ أَجْرٌ." [رَوَاهُ مُسْلِمٌ]

25 - Also on the authority of Abī Dharr (may Allāh be pleased with him):

Some people from amongst the Companions of the Messenger of Allāh (peace and blessings of Allāh be upon him) said to the Prophet (peace and blessings of Allāh be upon him): “O Messenger of Allāh, the affluent have made off with the rewards; they pray as we pray, they fast as we fast, and they give [much] in charity by virtue of their wealth.” He (peace and blessings of Allāh be upon him) said: “Has not Allāh made things for you to give in charity? Truly every tasbīḥah [saying: Subḥānallāh] is a charity, and every takbīrah [saying: Allāhu ‘Akbar] is a charity, and every taḥmīdah [saying: Alḥamdulillāh] is a charity, and every tahlīlah [saying: Lā ‘ilāha ‘illallāh] is a charity. And commanding the good is a charity, and forbidding an evil is a charity, and in the bud’i [sexual act] of each one of you there is a charity.” They said: “O Messenger of Allāh, when one of us fulfils his carnal desire will he have some reward for that?” He (peace and blessings of Allāh be upon him) said: “Do you not see that if he were to act upon it [his desire] in an unlawful manner then he would be deserving of punishment? Likewise, if he were to act upon it in a lawful manner then he will be deserving of a reward.” [Narrated by Muslim][30]

۞۞۞

---

(30) Ṣaḥīḥ Muslim (720 & 1006); Sunan Abī Dāwūd (1285, 1286 & 5243); Sunan At-Tirmidhī (1956); and Riyāḍ Us Ṣāliḥīn (11 1140 & 1432)

٢٦ - عَنْ أَبِي هُرَيْرَةَ رَضِيَ اللهُ عَنْهُ قَالَ: قَالَ رَسُولُ اللَّهِ صَلَّى اللَّهُ عَلَيْهِ وَسَلَّمَ: "كُلُّ سُلَامَى مِنْ النَّاسِ عَلَيْهِ صَدَقَةٌ، كُلَّ يَوْمٍ تَطْلُعُ فِيهِ الشَّمْسُ تَعْدِلُ بَيْنَ اثْنَيْنِ صَدَقَةٌ، وَتُعِينُ الرَّجُلَ فِي دَابَّتِهِ فَتَحْمِلُهُ عَلَيْهَا أَوْ تَرْفَعُ لَهُ عَلَيْهَا مَتَاعَهُ صَدَقَةٌ، وَالْكَلِمَةُ الطَّيِّبَةُ صَدَقَةٌ، وَبِكُلِّ خُطْوَةٍ تَمْشِيهَا إلَى الصَّلَاةِ صَدَقَةٌ، وَتُمِيطُ الْأَذَى عَنْ الطَّرِيقِ صَدَقَةٌ." [رَوَاهُ الْبُخَارِيُّ وَمُسْلِمٌ]

26 - On the authority of Abī Hurayrah (may Allāh be pleased with him) who said:

The Messenger of Allāh (peace and blessings of Allāh be upon him) said: "Every joint of a person must perform a charity each day that the sun rises: To judge justly between two people is a charity. To help a man with his mount, lifting him onto it or hoisting up his belongings onto it, is a charity. And the good word is a charity. And every step that you take towards the prayer is a charity, and removing a harmful object from the road is a charity." [Narrated by Bukhārī and Muslim][31]

۞۞۞

---

[31] Ṣaḥīḥ Al-Bukhārī (2707, 2891 & 2989); Ṣaḥīḥ Muslim (1009); and Riyāḍ Us Ṣāliḥīn (122 & 248)

٢٧ - عَنِ النَّوَّاسِ بْنِ سَمْعَانَ رَضِيَ اللهُ عَنْهُ عَنِ النَّبِيِّ صَلَّى اللهُ عَلَيْهِ وَسَلَّمَ قَالَ: "الْبِرُّ حُسْنُ الْخُلُقِ، وَالْإِثْمُ مَا حَاكَ فِي صَدْرِكَ، وَكَرِهْتَ أَنْ يَطَّلِعَ عَلَيْهِ النَّاسُ." [رَوَاهُ مُسْلِمٌ]

وَعَنْ وَابِصَةَ بْنِ مَعْبَدٍ رَضِيَ اللهُ عَنْهُ قَالَ: أَتَيْتُ رَسُولَ اللهِ صَلَّى اللهُ عَلَيْهِ وَسَلَّمَ فَقَالَ: "جِئْتَ تَسْأَلُ عَنِ الْبِرِّ؟ قُلْتُ: نَعَمْ. فَقَالَ: اسْتَفْتِ قَلْبَكَ، الْبِرُّ مَا اطْمَأَنَّتْ إِلَيْهِ النَّفْسُ، وَاطْمَأَنَّ إِلَيْهِ الْقَلْبُ، وَالْإِثْمُ مَا حَاكَ فِي النَّفْسِ وَتَرَدَّدَ فِي الصَّدْرِ، وَإِنْ أَفْتَاكَ النَّاسُ وَأَفْتَوْكَ."

حَدِيثٌ حَسَنٌ، رَوَيْنَاهُ فِي مُسْنَدَيِ الْإِمَامَيْنِ أَحْمَدَ بْنِ حَنْبَلٍ، وَالدَّارِمِيِّ بِإِسْنَادٍ حَسَنٍ.

27 - On the authority of An-Nawās Bin Sam'ān (may Allāh be pleased with him), that the Prophet (peace and blessings of Allāh be upon him) said:

"Righteousness is in good character, and wrongdoing is that which wavers in your soul, and which you dislike people finding out about." [Narrated by Muslim][32]

And on the authority of Wābiṣah Bin Ma'bad (may Allāh be pleased with him) who said:
I came to the Messenger of Allāh (peace and blessings of Allāh be upon him) and he (peace and blessings of Allāh be upon him) said: "You have come to ask about righteousness." I said: "Yes." He (peace and blessings of Allāh be upon him) said: "Consult your heart. Righteousness is that about which the soul feels at ease and the heart attains tranquility. And wrongdoing is that which wavers in the soul and causes uneasiness in the breast, even though people have repeatedly given their legal opinion [in its favor]."

A ḥasan ḥadīth transmitted from the Musnads of the two Imāms, Aḥmad Bin Ḥanbal and Ad- Dārimī, with a ḥasan chain of authorities.[33]

---

(32) Ṣaḥīḥ Muslim (2553); Sunan At-Tirmidhī (2389); and Riyāḍ Us Ṣāliḥīn (590 & 624)
(33) Musnad Aḥmad (Ḥadīth no. 17999 (pg. 523-524, vol 29), no. 18001 (pg. 527-529, vol 29) & no. 18006 (pg. 532-533, v
29)); Sunan Ad-Dārimī (Ḥadīth no. 2533 (pg. 197, vol 2)); and Riyāḍ Us Ṣāliḥīn (591)

٢٨ - عَنْ أَبِي نَجِيحٍ الْعِرْبَاضِ بْنِ سَارِيَةَ رَضِيَ اللَّهُ عَنْهُ قَالَ: "وَعَظَنَا رَسُولُ اللَّهِ صَلَّى اللَّهُ عَلَيْهِ وَسَلَّمَ مَوْعِظَةً وَجِلَتْ مِنْهَا الْقُلُوبُ، وَذَرَفَتْ مِنْهَا الْعُيُونُ، فَقُلْنَا: يَا رَسُولَ اللَّهِ! كَأَنَّهَا مَوْعِظَةُ مُوَدِّعٍ فَأَوْصِنَا، قَالَ: أُوصِيكُمْ بِتَقْوَى اللَّهِ، وَالسَّمْعِ وَالطَّاعَةِ وَإِنْ تَأَمَّرَ عَلَيْكُمْ عَبْدٌ، فَإِنَّهُ مَنْ يَعِشْ مِنْكُمْ فَسَيَرَى اخْتِلَافًا كَثِيرًا، فَعَلَيْكُمْ بِسُنَّتِي وَسُنَّةِ الْخُلَفَاءِ الرَّاشِدِينَ الْمَهْدِيِّينَ، عَضُّوا عَلَيْهَا بِالنَّوَاجِذِ، وَإِيَّاكُمْ وَمُحْدَثَاتِ الْأُمُورِ؛ فَإِنَّ كُلَّ مُحْدَثَةٍ بِدْعَةٌ، وَكُلَّ بِدْعَةٍ ضَلَالَةٌ."

[رَوَاهُ أَبُو دَاوُدَ، وَالتِّرْمِذِيُّ – وَقَالَ: حَدِيثٌ حَسَنٌ صَحِيحٌ]

28 - On the authority of Abī Najīḥ Al-'Irbāḍ Bin Sāriyah (may Allāh be pleased with him) who said:

The Messenger of Allāh (peace and blessings of Allāh be upon him) gave us a sermon by which our hearts were filled with fear and tears came to our eyes. So we said: "O Messenger of Allāh! It is as though this is a farewell sermon, so counsel us." He (peace and blessings of Allāh be upon him) said: "I counsel you to have taqwā (fear) of Allāh, and to listen and obey [your leader], even if a slave were to become your 'amīr. Verily he among you who lives long will see great controversy, so you must keep to my Sunnah and to the Sunnah of the Khulafā' Ar-Rāshidīn (the rightly guided caliphs), those who guide to the right way. Cling to it stubbornly [literally: with your molar teeth]. Beware of newly invented matters [in the religion], for verily every bid'ah (innovation) is misguidance."

[Narrated by Abū Dāwūd and At-Tirmidhī, who said that it is a ḥasan ṣaḥīḥ ḥadīth][34]

---

4) Sunan Abī Dāwūd (4607); Sunan At-Tirmidhī (2676); Sunan Ibn Mājah (EN [42 & 43] – AR [44 & 45]); and Riyāḍ Us Ṣāliḥīn 57, 456 & 702)

٢٩ - عَنْ مُعَاذِ بْنِ جَبَلٍ رَضِيَ اللّٰهُ عَنْهُ قَالَ: قُلْتُ يَا رَسُولَ اللّٰهِ! أَخْبِرْنِي بِعَمَلٍ يُدْخِلْنِي الْجَنَّةَ وَيُبَاعِدُنِي مِنَ النَّارِ، قَالَ: "لَقَدْ سَأَلْتَ عَنْ عَظِيمٍ، وَإِنَّهُ لَيَسِيرٌ عَلَى مَنْ يَسَّرَهُ اللّٰهُ عَلَيْهِ: تَعْبُدُ اللّٰهَ لَا تُشْرِكُ بِهِ شَيْئًا، وَتُقِيمُ الصَّلَاةَ، وَتُؤْتِي الزَّكَاةَ، وَتَصُومُ رَمَضَانَ، وَتَحُجُّ الْبَيْتَ، ثُمَّ قَالَ: أَلَا أَدُلُّكَ عَلَى أَبْوَابِ الْخَيْرِ؟ الصَّوْمُ جُنَّةٌ، وَالصَّدَقَةُ تُطْفِئُ الْخَطِيئَةَ كَمَا يُطْفِئُ الْمَاءُ النَّارَ، وَصَلَاةُ الرَّجُلِ فِي جَوْفِ اللَّيْلِ، ثُمَّ تَلَا: ﴿تَتَجَافَىٰ جُنُوبُهُمْ عَنِ الْمَضَاجِعِ يَدْعُونَ رَبَّهُمْ خَوْفًا وَطَمَعًا وَمِمَّا رَزَقْنَاهُمْ يُنْفِقُونَ ۝ فَلَا تَعْلَمُ نَفْسٌ مَّا أُخْفِيَ لَهُم مِّن قُرَّةِ أَعْيُنٍ جَزَاءً بِمَا كَانُوا يَعْمَلُونَ﴾ ثُمَّ قَالَ: أَلَا أُخْبِرُكَ بِرَأْسِ الْأَمْرِ وَعَمُودِهِ وَذِرْوَةِ سَنَامِهِ؟ قُلْتُ: بَلَى يَا رَسُولَ اللّٰهِ. قَالَ: رَأْسُ الْأَمْرِ الْإِسْلَامُ، وَعَمُودُهُ الصَّلَاةُ، وَذِرْوَةُ سَنَامِهِ الْجِهَادُ، ثُمَّ قَالَ: أَلَا أُخْبِرُكَ بِمَلَاكِ ذَلِكَ كُلِّهِ؟ فَقُلْتُ: بَلَى يَا رَسُولَ اللّٰهِ! فَأَخَذَ بِلِسَانِهِ وَقَالَ: كُفَّ عَلَيْكَ هَذَا. قُلْتُ: يَا نَبِيَّ اللّٰهِ وَإِنَّا لَمُؤَاخَذُونَ بِمَا نَتَكَلَّمُ بِهِ؟ فَقَالَ: ثَكِلَتْكَ أُمُّكَ وَهَلْ يَكُبُّ النَّاسَ فِي النَّارِ عَلَى وُجُوهِهِمْ - أَوْ قَالَ عَلَى مَنَاخِرِهِمْ - إِلَّا حَصَائِدُ أَلْسِنَتِهِمْ؟"

[رَوَاهُ التِّرْمِذِيُّ - وَقَالَ: حَدِيثٌ حَسَنٌ صَحِيحٌ]

29 - On the authority of Mu'ādh Bin Jabal (may Allāh be pleased with him) who said:

I said: "O Messenger of Allāh, tell me of an act which will take me into Paradise and will keep me away from the Hellfire." He (peace and blessings of Allāh be upon him) said: "You have asked me about a great matter, yet it is easy for him for whom Allāh makes it easy: Worship Allāh, without associating any partners with Him; establish the prayer; pay the Zakāh; fast in Ramaḍān; and make the pilgrimage to the House." Then he (peace and blessings of Allāh be upon him) said: "Shall I not guide you towards the means of goodness? Fasting is a shield; charity wipes away sin as water extinguishes fire; and the praying of a man in the depths of the night." Then he (peace and blessings of Allāh be upon him) recited: ﴿[Those] who forsake their beds, to invoke their Lord in fear and hope, and they spend (charity in Allāh's cause) out of what We have bestowed on them ۝ No person knows what is kept hidden for them of joy as a reward for what they used to do﴾ [35](36) Then he (peace and blessings of Allāh be upon him) said: "Shall I not inform you of the head of the matter, its pillar and its peak?" I said: "Yes, O Messenger of Allāh." He (peace and blessings of Allāh be upon him) said: "The head of the matter is Islām, its pillar is the prayer and its peak is jihād." Then he (peace and blessings of Allāh be upon him) said: "Shall I not tell you of the foundation of all of that?" I said: "Yes, O Messenger of Allāh." So he took hold of his tongue and said: "Restrain this." I said: "O Prophet of Allāh, will we be taken to account for what we say with it?" He (peace and blessings of Allāh be upon him) said: "May your mother be bereaved of you, O Mu'ādh! Is there anything that throws people into the Hellfire upon their faces — or on their noses — except the harvest of their tongues?"

---

(35) Al-Qur'ān: Chapter 32 (As-Sajdah), Verse: 16-17
(36) Editor: The original text mentioned only the starting and the ending of the verse. But, we have added the full verse with its translation [Saheeh International].

[It was narrated by At-Tirmidhī, who said it is a ḥasan ṣaḥīḥ ḥadīth][37]

✪✪✪

---

(37) Sunan An-Nasā'ī (2224 [2226], 2225 [2227] & 2226 [2228]); Sunan At-Tirmidhī (2616); Sunan Ibn Mājah (3973); and Riyāḍ Ṣāliḥīn (1522)

٣٠ - عَنْ أَبِي ثَعْلَبَةَ الْخُشَنِيِّ جُرْثُومِ بن نَاشِرٍ رَضِيَ اللهُ عَنْهُ عَنْ رَسُولِ اللَّهِ صَلَّى اللَّهُ عَلَيْهِ وَسَلَّمَ قَالَ: "إنَّ اللَّهَ تَعَالَى فَرَضَ فَرَائِضَ فَلَا تُضَيِّعُوهَا، وَحَدَّ حُدُودًا فَلَا تَعْتَدُوهَا، وَحَرَّمَ أَشْيَاءَ فَلَا تَنْتَهِكُوهَا، وَسَكَتَ عَنْ أَشْيَاءَ رَحْمَةً لَكُمْ غَيْرَ نِسْيَانٍ فَلَا تَبْحَثُوا عَنْهَا."

[حَدِيثٌ حَسَنٌ، رَوَاهُ الدَّارَقُطْنِيّ، وَغَيْرُهُ]

30 - On the authority of Abī Tha'labah Al-Kushanī Khurthūm Bin Nāshir (may Allāh be pleased with him), that the Messenger of Allāh (peace and blessings of Allāh be upon him) said:

"Verily Allāh ta'ālā has laid down religious obligations (farā'iḍ), so do not neglect them; and He has set limits, so do not overstep them; and He has forbidden some things, so do not violate them; and He has remained silent about some things, out of compassion for you, not out of forgetfulness, so do not go seeking them."

[A ḥasan ḥadīth narrated by Ad-Dāraquṭnī and others](38)

---

(38) Sunan Ad-Dāraquṭnī (Ḥadīth no. 4396 (pg. 325-326, vol 5)); and Riyāḍ Us Ṣāliḥīn (1832)

٣١ - عَنْ أَبِي الْعَبَّاسِ سَهْلِ بْنِ سَعْدٍ السَّاعِدِيّ رَضِيَ اللهُ عَنْهُ قَالَ: جَاءَ رَجُلٌ إِلَى النَّبِيِّ صَلَّى اللهُ عَلَيْهِ وَسَلَّمَ فَقَالَ: يَا رَسُولَ اللهِ! دُلَّنِي عَلَى عَمَلٍ إِذَا عَمِلْتُهُ أَحَبَّنِي اللهُ وَأَحَبَّنِي النَّاسُ؛ فَقَالَ: "ازْهَدْ فِي الدُّنْيَا يُحِبَّك اللهُ، وَازْهَدْ فِيمَا عِنْدَ النَّاسِ يُحِبَّك النَّاسُ."

[حَدِيثٌ حَسَنٌ، رَوَاهُ ابْنُ مَاجَهْ، وَغَيْرُهُ بِأَسَانِيدَ حَسَنَةٍ]

31 - On the authority of Abī Al-'Abbās Sahl Bin Sa'd As-Sā'idī (may Allāh be pleased with him) who said:

A man came to the Prophet (peace and blessings of Allāh be upon him) and said: "O Messenger of Allāh, direct me to an act which, if I do it, [will cause] Allāh to love me and the people to love me." So he (peace and blessings of Allāh be upon him) said: "Renounce the world and Allāh will love you, and renounce what the people possess and the people will love you."

[A ḥasan ḥadīth narrated by Ibn Mājah and others with ḥasan chain of authorities](39)

۞ ۞ ۞

(39) Sunan Ibn Mājah (EN [4102] – AR [4241]); and Riyāḍ Us Ṣāliḥīn (472)

٣٢ - عَنْ أَبِي سَعِيدٍ سَعْدِ بْنِ مَالِكِ بْنِ سِنَانٍ الْخُدْرِيِّ رَضِيَ اللهُ عَنْهُ أَنَّ رَسُولَ اللَّهِ صَلَّى اللَّهُ عَلَيْهِ وَسَلَّمَ قَالَ: "لَا ضَرَرَ وَلَا ضِرَارَ."

حَدِيثٌ حَسَنٌ، رَوَاهُ ابْنُ مَاجَهْ، وَالدَّارَقُطْنِيّ، وَغَيْرُهُمَا مُسْنَدًا. وَرَوَاهُ مَالِكٌ فِي الْمُوَطَّإِ عَنْ عَمْرِو بْنِ يَحْيَى عَنْ أَبِيهِ عَنْ النَّبِيِّ صَلَّى اللَّهُ عَلَيْهِ وَسَلَّمَ مُرْسَلًا، فَأَسْقَطَ أَبَا سَعِيدٍ، وَلَهُ طُرُقٌ يُقَوِّي بَعْضُهَا بَعْضًا.

32 - On the authority of Abī Sa'īd Sa'd Bin Mālik Bin Sinān Al-Khudrī (may Allāh be pleased with him), that the Messenger of Allāh (peace and blessings of Allāh be upon him) said:

"There should be neither harming (ḍarara) nor reciprocating harm (ḍirār)."

A ḥasan ḥadīth narrated by Ibn Mājah, Ad-Dāraquṭnī and others as a Musnad ḥadīth. It was also narrated by Mālik in Al-Muwaṭṭa' in mursal form, from 'Amr Bin Yaḥyā, from his father from the Prophet (peace and blessings of Allāh be upon him), but leaving Abī Sa'īd from the chain. And it has other chain of authorities that strengthen one another.(40)

✡✡✡

---

(40) Sunan Ibn Mājah (2341); Sunan Ad-Dāraquṭnī (Ḥadīth no. 4541 (pg. 408, vol 5)); Muwaṭṭa' Malik (Ḥadīth no. 1503 (pg. 567, vol 1)); and Riyāḍ Us Ṣāliḥīn (308, 314 & 706)

٣٣ - عَنْ ابْنِ عَبَّاسٍ رَضِيَ اللَّهُ عَنْهُمَا أَنَّ رَسُولَ اللَّهِ صَلَّى اللَّهُ عَلَيْهِ وَسَلَّمَ قَالَ: "لَوْ يُعْطَى النَّاسُ بِدَعْوَاهُمْ لَادَّعَى رِجَالٌ أَمْوَالَ قَوْمٍ وَدِمَاءَهُمْ، وَلَكِنَّ الْبَيِّنَةَ عَلَى الْمُدَّعِي، وَالْيَمِينَ عَلَى مَنْ أَنْكَرَ."

[حَدِيثٌ حَسَنٌ، رَوَاهُ الْبَيْهَقِيّ، وَغَيْرُهُ هَكَذَا، وَبَعْضُهُ فِي الصَّحِيحَيْنِ]

33 - On the authority of Ibn 'Abbās (may Allāh be pleased with them both), that the Messenger of Allāh (peace and blessings of Allāh be upon him) said:

"Were people to be given everything that they claimed, men would [unjustly] claim the wealth and lives of [other] people. But, the burden of proof is upon the claimant, and the taking of an oath is upon him who denies."

[A ḥasan ḥadīth narrated by Al-Bayhaqī and others in this form(41), and part of it is in the two ṣaḥīḥs(42)]

---

(41) Sunan Al-Kubrā (Ḥadīth no. 21197-21203 (pg. 426-427, vol 10))
(42) Ṣaḥīḥ Al-Bukhārī (2514, 2668 & 4552); Ṣaḥīḥ Muslim (1711); Sunan Abī Dāwūd (3619); Sunan At-Tirmidhī (1342); and Sunan Ibn Mājah (2321)

٣٤ - عَنْ أَبِي سَعِيدٍ الْخُدْرِيِّ رَضِيَ اللهُ عَنْهُ قَالَ: سَمِعْت رَسُولَ اللَّهِ صَلَّى اللَّهُ عَلَيْهِ وَسَلَّمَ يَقُولُ: "مَنْ رَأَى مِنْكُمْ مُنْكَرًا فَلْيُغَيِّرْهُ بِيَدِهِ، فَإِنْ لَمْ يَسْتَطِعْ فَبِلِسَانِهِ، فَإِنْ لَمْ يَسْتَطِعْ فَبِقَلْبِهِ، وَذَلِكَ أَضْعَفُ الْإِيمَانِ." [رَوَاهُ مُسْلِمٌ]

34 - On the authority of Abī Sa'īd Al-Khudrī (may Allāh be pleased with him) who said:

I heard the Messenger of Allāh (peace and blessings of Allāh be upon him) say: "Whoever of you sees an evil, let him change it with his hand; and if he is not able to do so, then [let him change it] with his tongue; and if he is not able to do so, then with his heart and that is the weakest of faith." [Narrated by Muslim](43)

✡✡✡

---

(43) Ṣaḥīḥ Muslim (49); Sunan Abī Dāwūd (1140 & 4340); Sunan An-Nasā'ī (5008 [5011] & 5009 [5012]); Sunan At-Tirmid (2172); Sunan Ibn Mājah (EN [1275] – AR [1334] & 4013); and Riyāḍ Us Ṣāliḥīn (184)

٣٥ - عَنْ أَبِي هُرَيْرَةَ رَضِيَ اللهُ عَنْهُ قَالَ: قَالَ رَسُولُ اللَّهِ صَلَّى اللَّهُ عَلَيْهِ وَسَلَّمَ: "لَا تَحَاسَدُوا، وَلَا تَنَاجَشُوا، وَلَا تَبَاغَضُوا، وَلَا تَدَابَرُوا، وَلَا يَبِعْ بَعْضُكُمْ عَلَى بَيْعِ بَعْضٍ، وَكُونُوا عِبَادَ اللَّهِ إِخْوَانًا، الْمُسْلِمُ أَخُو الْمُسْلِمِ، لَا يَظْلِمُهُ، وَلَا يَخْذُلُهُ، وَلَا يَكْذِبُهُ، وَلَا يَحْقِرُهُ، التَّقْوَى هَاهُنَا، وَيُشِيرُ إِلَى صَدْرِهِ ثَلَاثَ مَرَّاتٍ، بِحَسْبِ امْرِئٍ مِنْ الشَّرِّ أَنْ يَحْقِرَ أَخَاهُ الْمُسْلِمَ، كُلُّ الْمُسْلِمِ عَلَى الْمُسْلِمِ حَرَامٌ: دَمُهُ وَمَالُهُ وَعِرْضُهُ." [رَوَاهُ مُسْلِمٌ]

35 - On the authority of Abī Hurayrah (may Allāh be pleased with him) who said:

The Messenger of Allāh (peace and blessings of Allāh be upon him) said: "Do not envy one another, and do not inflate prices for one another, and do not hate one another, and do not turn away from one another, and do not undercut one another in trade, but [rather] be slaves of Allāh and brothers [amongst yourselves]. A Muslim is the brother of a Muslim: He does not oppress him, nor does he fail him, nor does he lie to him, nor does he hold him in contempt. Taqwā (piety) is right here [and he pointed to his chest three times]. It is evil enough for a man to hold his brother Muslim in contempt. The whole of a Muslim is inviolable for another Muslim: His blood, his property, and his honour." [Narrated by Muslim](44)

۞۞۞

---

4) Ṣaḥīḥ Muslim (2564); and Riyāḍ Us Ṣāliḥīn (235)

is recorded with different versions in Ṣaḥīḥ Al-Bukhārī, Ṣaḥīḥ Muslim, Sunan Abī Dāwūd, Sunan An-Nasā'ī, Sunan At-rmidhī, Sunan Ibn Mājah, and Riyāḍ Us Ṣāliḥīn, which will be added in the next edition with a detailed takhrīj in shā Allāh.

٣٦ - عَنْ أَبِي هُرَيْرَةَ رَضِيَ اللهُ عَنْهُ عَنْ النَّبِيِّ صَلَّى اللَّهُ عَلَيْهِ وَسَلَّمَ قَالَ: "مَنْ نَفَّسَ عَنْ مُؤْمِنٍ كُرْبَةً مِنْ كُرَبِ الدُّنْيَا نَفَّسَ اللَّهُ عَنْهُ كُرْبَةً مِنْ كُرَبِ يَوْمِ الْقِيَامَةِ، وَمَنْ يَسَّرَ عَلَى مُعْسِرٍ، يَسَّرَ اللَّهُ عَلَيْهِ فِي الدُّنْيَا وَالْآخِرَةِ، وَمَنْ سَتَرَ مُسْلِما سَتَرَهُ اللهُ فِي الدُّنْيَا وَالْآخِرَةِ ، وَاللَّهُ فِي عَوْنِ الْعَبْدِ مَا كَانَ الْعَبْدُ فِي عَوْنِ أَخِيهِ، وَمَنْ سَلَكَ طَرِيقًا يَلْتَمِسُ فِيهِ عِلْمًا سَهَّلَ اللَّهُ لَهُ بِهِ طَرِيقًا إلَى الْجَنَّةِ، وَمَا اجْتَمَعَ قَوْمٌ فِي بَيْتٍ مِنْ بُيُوتِ اللَّهِ يَتْلُونَ كِتَابَ اللَّهِ، وَيَتَدَارَسُونَهُ فِيمَا بَيْنَهُمْ؛ إلَّا نَزَلَتْ عَلَيْهِمْ السَّكِينَةُ، وَغَشِيَتْهُمْ الرَّحْمَةُ، وَ حَفَّتْهُمْ الْمَلَائِكَة، وَذَكَرَهُمْ اللَّهُ فِيمَنْ عِنْدَهُ، وَمَنْ بَطَّأَ بِهِ عَمَلُهُ لَمْ يُسْرِعْ بِهِ نَسَبُهُ." [رَوَاهُ مُسْلِمٌ بِهَذَا اللَّفْظِ]

36 - On the authority of Abī Hurayrah (may Allāh be pleased with him), that the Prophet (peace and blessings of Allāh be upon him) said:

"Whoever removes a worldly grief from a believer, Allāh will remove from him one of the griefs of the Day of Resurrection. And whoever alleviates the need of a needy person, Allāh will alleviate his needs in this world and the Hereafter. Whoever shields [or hides the misdeeds of] a Muslim, Allāh will shield him in this world and the Hereafter. And Allāh will aid His slave so long as he aids his brother. And whoever follows a path to seek knowledge therein, Allāh will make easy for him a path to Paradise. No people gather together in one of the Houses of Allāh, reciting the Book of Allāh and studying it among themselves, except that sakīnah (tranquility) descends upon them, and mercy envelops them, and the angels surround them, and Allāh mentions them amongst those who are with Him. And whoever is slowed down by his actions, will not be hastened forward by his lineage." [Narrated by Muslim with these words][45]

۞۞۞

(45) **Ṣaḥīḥ Muslim** (2699 & 2700); **Sunan Abī Dāwūd** (1455, 3643 & 4946); **Sunan At-Tirmidhī** (1425, 1930, 3378 & EN [2945] AR [3197]); **Sunan Ibn Mājah** (EN [225 & 2544] – AR [230 & 2641] & 3791); **and Riyāḍ Us Ṣāliḥīn** (240 & 245)

٣٧ - عَنْ ابْنِ عَبَّاسٍ رَضِيَ اللَّهُ عَنْهُمَا عَنْ رَسُولِ اللَّهِ صَلَّى اللَّهُ عَلَيْهِ وَسَلَّمَ فِيمَا يَرْوِيهِ عَنْ رَبِّهِ تَبَارَكَ وَتَعَالَى، قَالَ: "إنَّ اللَّهَ كَتَبَ الْحَسَنَاتِ وَالسَّيِّئَاتِ، ثُمَّ بَيَّنَ ذَلِكَ، فَمَنْ هَمَّ بِحَسَنَةٍ فَلَمْ يَعْمَلْهَا كَتَبَهَا اللَّهُ عِنْدَهُ حَسَنَةً كَامِلَةً، وَإِنْ هَمَّ بِهَا فَعَمِلَهَا كَتَبَهَا اللَّهُ عِنْدَهُ عَشْرَ حَسَنَاتٍ إلَى سَبْعِمِائَةِ ضِعْفٍ إلَى أَضْعَافٍ كَثِيرَةٍ، وَإِنْ هَمَّ بِسَيِّئَةٍ فَلَمْ يَعْمَلْهَا كَتَبَهَا اللَّهُ عِنْدَهُ حَسَنَةً كَامِلَةً، وَإِنْ هَمَّ بِهَا فَعَمِلَهَا كَتَبَهَا اللَّهُ سَيِّئَةً وَاحِدَةً." [رَوَاهُ الْبُخَارِيُّ وَمُسْلِمٌ فِي صَحِيحَيْهِمَا بِهَذِهِ الْحُرُوفِ]

37 - On the authority of Ibn ‘Abbās (may Allāh be pleased with them both), from the Messenger of Allāh (peace and blessings of Allāh be upon him), from among the sayings that he related from his Lord (Glorified and Exalted be He) is that He said:

“Verily Allāh has written down the good deeds and the evil deeds, and then explained it [by saying]: Whosoever intended to perform a good deed, but did not do it, then Allāh writes it down with Himself as a complete good deed. And if he intended to perform it and then did perform it, then Allāh writes it down with Himself as from ten good deeds up to seven hundred times, up to many times multiplied. And if he intended to perform an evil deed, but did not do it, then Allāh writes it down with Himself as a complete good deed. And if he intended it [i.e., the evil deed] and then performed it, then Allāh writes it down as one evil deed.” [Narrated by Bukhārī and Muslim in their two ṣaḥīḥs with these wordings](46)

۞۞۞

---

(46) Ṣaḥīḥ Al-Bukhārī (6491); Ṣaḥīḥ Muslim (131); and Riyāḍ Us Ṣāliḥīn (11)

٣٨ - عَنْ أَبِي هُرَيْرَةَ رَضِيَ اللهُ عَنْهُ قَالَ: قَالَ رَسُولُ اللَّهِ صَلَّى اللهُ عَلَيْهِ وَسَلَّمَ إِنَّ اللَّهَ تَعَالَى قَالَ: "مَنْ عَادَى لِي وَلِيًّا فَقَدْ آذَنْتهُ بِالْحَرْبِ، وَمَا تَقَرَّبَ إِلَيَّ عَبْدِي بِشَيْءٍ أَحَبَّ إِلَيَّ مِمَّا افْتَرَضْتُهُ عَلَيْهِ، وَلَا يَزَالُ عَبْدِي يَتَقَرَّبُ إِلَيَّ بِالنَّوَافِلِ حَتَّى أُحِبَّهُ، فَإِذَا أَحْبَبْتُهُ كُنْت سَمْعَهُ الَّذِي يَسْمَعُ بِهِ، وَبَصَرَهُ الَّذِي يُبْصِرُ بِهِ، وَيَدَهُ الَّتِي يَبْطِشُ بِهَا، وَرِجْلَهُ الَّتِي يَمْشِي بِهَا، وَلَئِنْ سَأَلَنِي لَأُعْطِيَنَّهُ، وَلَئِنْ اسْتَعَاذَنِي لَأُعِيذَنَّهُ." [رَوَاهُ الْبُخَارِيُّ]

38 - On the authority of Abī Hurayrah (may Allāh be pleased with him) who said:

The Messenger of Allāh (peace and blessings of Allāh be upon him) said: "Verily Allāh ta'ālā has said: 'Whosoever shows enmity to a walī (friend) of Mine, then I have declared war against him. And My servant does not draw near to Me with anything more loved to Me than the religious duties I have obligated upon him. And My servant continues to draw near to me with nawāfil (supererogatory deeds) until I Love him. When I Love him, I am his hearing with which he hears, and his sight with which he sees, and his hand with which he strikes, and his foot with which he walks. Were he to ask [something] of Me, I would surely give it to him; and were he to seek refuge with Me, I would surely grant him refuge.'" [Narrated by Bukhārī][47]

۞۞۞

(47) Ṣaḥīḥ Al-Bukhārī (6502); and Riyāḍ Us Ṣāliḥīn (95 & 386)

٣٩ - عَنْ ابْنِ عَبَّاسٍ رَضِيَ اللَّهُ عَنْهُمَا أَنَّ رَسُولَ اللَّهِ صَلَّى اللَّهُ عَلَيْهِ وَسَلَّمَ قَالَ: "إنَّ اللَّهَ تَجَاوَزَ لِي عَنْ أُمَّتِي الْخَطَأَ وَالنِّسْيَانَ وَمَا اسْتُكْرِهُوا عَلَيْهِ."

[حَدِيثٌ حَسَنٌ، رَوَاهُ ابْنُ مَاجَهْ، وَالْبَيْهَقِيّ وَغَيْرُهُمَا]

39 - On the authority of Ibn 'Abbās (may Allāh be pleased with them both), that the Messenger of Allāh (peace and blessings of Allāh be upon him) said:

"Verily Allāh has pardoned [or been lenient with] for me my ummah: Their mistakes, their forgetfulness, and that which they have been forced to do under duress."

[A ḥasan ḥadīth narrated by Ibn Mājah, Al-Bayhaqī and others](48)

---

(48) **Sunan Ibn Mājah** (EN [2045] – AR [2123]); and **Sunan Al-Kubrā** (Ḥadīth no. 15094 (pg. 584, vol 7))

٤٠ - عَنْ ابْن عُمَرَ رَضِيَ اللَّهُ عَنْهُمَا قَالَ: أَخَذَ رَسُولُ اللَّهِ صَلَّى اللَّهُ عَلَيْهِ وَسَلَّمَ بِمَنْكِبِي، وَقَالَ: "كُنْ فِي الدُّنْيَا كَأَنَّكَ غَرِيبٌ أَوْ عَابِرُ سَبِيلٍ."

وَكَانَ ابْنُ عُمَرَ رَضِيَ اللَّهُ عَنْهُمَا يَقُولُ: "إذَا أَمْسَيْتَ فَلَا تَنْتَظِرْ الصَّبَاحَ، وَإِذَا أَصْبَحْتَ فَلَا تَنْتَظِرْ الْمَسَاءَ، وَخُذْ مِنْ صِحَّتِك لِمَرَضِك، وَمِنْ حَيَاتِك لِمَوْتِك." [رَوَاهُ الْبُخَارِيُّ]

40 - On the authority of Ibn 'Umar (may Allāh be pleased with them both), who said:

The Messenger of Allāh (peace and blessings of Allāh be upon him) took me by the shoulder and said: "Be in this world as though you were a stranger or a wayfarer."

And Ibn 'Umar (may Allāh be pleased with them both) used to say: "In the evening do not expect [to live until] the morning, and in the morning do not expect [to live until] the evening. Take [advantage of] your health before times of sickness, and [take advantage of] your life before your death." [Narrated by Bukhārī][49]

✪✪✪

(49) Ṣaḥīḥ Al-Bukhārī (6416); Sunan At-Tirmidhī (2333); Sunan Ibn Mājah (EN [4114] – AR [4253]); and Riyāḍ Us Ṣāliḥīn (4[illegible] & 574)

٤١ - عَنْ أَبِي مُحَمَّدٍ عَبْدِ اللَّهِ بْنِ عَمْرِو بْنِ الْعَاصِ رَضِيَ اللَّهُ عَنْهُمَا، قَالَ: قَالَ رَسُولُ اللَّهِ صَلَّى اللَّهُ عَلَيْهِ وَسَلَّمَ: "لَا يُؤْمِنُ أَحَدُكُمْ حَتَّى يَكُونَ هَوَاهُ تَبَعًا لِمَا جِئْتُ بِهِ."

[حَدِيثٌ حَسَنٌ صَحِيحٌ، رَوَيْنَاهُ فِي كِتَابِ "الْحُجَّةِ" بِإِسْنَادٍ صَحِيحٍ]

41 - On the authority of Abī Muḥammad ‘Abd Allāh Bin ‘Amr Bin Al-‘Āṣ (may Allāh be pleased with them both) who said:

The Messenger of Allāh (peace and blessings of Allāh be upon him) said: “None of you [truly] believes until his desires are subservient to that which I have brought.”

[Ḥadīth is ḥasan ṣaḥīḥ and we have related it in Kitāb “Al-Ḥujjah” with a ṣaḥīḥ chain of authorities](50)

۞۞۞

---

(50) Kitāb Al-Ḥujjah (Ḥadīth no. 103 (pg. 251-252, vol 1))

٤٢ - عَنْ أَنَسِ بْنِ مَالِكٍ رَضِيَ اللهُ عَنْهُ قَالَ: سَمِعْت رَسُولَ اللَّهِ صَلَّى اللَّهُ عَلَيْهِ وَسَلَّمَ يَقُولُ: قَالَ اللَّهُ تَعَالَى: "يَا ابْنَ آدَمَ! إنَّكَ مَا دَعَوْتنِي وَرَجَوْتنِي غَفَرْتُ لَك عَلَى مَا كَانَ مِنْك وَلَا أُبَالِي، يَا ابْنَ آدَمَ! لَوْ بَلَغَتْ ذُنُوبُك عَنَانَ السَّمَاءِ ثُمَّ اسْتَغْفَرْتنِي غَفَرْتُ لَك وَلاَ أُبَالِي، يَا ابْنَ آدَمَ! إنَّك لَوْ أَتَيْتنِي بِقُرَابِ الْأَرْضِ خَطَايَا ثُمَّ لَقِيتنِي لَا تُشْرِكُ بِي شَيْئًا لَأَتَيْتُك بِقُرَابِهَا مَغْفِرَةً."

[رَوَاهُ التِّرْمِذِيُّ – وَقَالَ: حَدِيثٌ حَسَنٌ صَحِيحٌ]

42 - On the authority of Anas Bin Mālik (may Allāh be pleased with him) who said:

I heard the Messenger of Allāh (peace and blessings of Allāh be upon him) say: "Allāh the Almighty has said: 'O Son of Ādam, as long as you invoke Me and ask of Me, I shall forgive you for what you have done, and I shall not mind. O Son of Ādam, were your sins to reach the clouds of the sky and you then asked forgiveness from Me, I would forgive you. O Son of Ādam, were you to come to Me with sins nearly as great as the Earth, and were you then to face Me, ascribing no partner to Me, I would bring you forgiveness nearly as great as it [too].'"

[Narrated by At-Tirmidhī, and he said that it is a ḥasan ṣaḥīḥ ḥadīth][51]

---

(51) Sunan At-Tirmidhī (3540); and Riyāḍ Us Ṣāliḥīn (442 & 1878)

Publishers of books[52] used as reference:

- **Ṣaḥīḥ Al-Bukhārī:** Dārussalām [53]
- **Ṣaḥīḥ Muslim:** Dārussalām [54]
- **Sunan Abī Dāwūd:** Dārussalām [55] and Maktabah Al-Ma'ārif [56]
- **Sunan An-Nasā'ī:** Dārussalām [57] and Maktabah Al-Ma'ārif [58]
- **Sunan At-Tirmidhī:** [59] Dārussalām [60] and Maktabah Al-Ma'ārif [61]
- **Sunan Ibn Mājah:** Dārussalām [62] and Maktabah Al-Ma'ārif [63]
- **Sunan Ad-Dārimī:** Dār Al-Kutub Al-'Ilmiyah [64]
- **Muwaṭṭa' Mālik:** Ar-Resālah Publishers [65]
- **Musnad Aḥmad:** Ar-Resālah Publishers [66]
- **Riyād Us Ṣāliḥīn:** Ar-Resālah Publishers [67]
- **Sunan Ad-Dāraquṭnī:** Ar-Resālah Publishers [68]
- **Sunan Al-Kubrā:** Dār Al-Kutub Al-'Ilmiyah [69]
- **Kitāb Al-Ḥujjah:** Dār Ur-Rāyah [70]

Notes:

- The numbers in square brackets when quoting from Sunan An-Nasā'ī refers to the ḥadīth number according to Dārussalām's publication.

52) Editor: All the books referred are limited to Arabic versions.
53) Edition [2nd]; Published [1419H]; Vol [1]
54) Edition [2nd]; Published [1421H]; Vol [1]
55) Published [1430H]; Vol [1]; Researcher [Ḥāfiz Abū Ṭāhir Zubāir 'Alī Za'ī]
56) ISBN [9-87-769-9960]; Edition [2nd]; Published [1427H]; Vol [1]; Researcher [Shaykh Muḥammad Nāṣiruddīn Al-Albānī]
57) Published [1430H]; Vol [1]; Researcher [Ḥāfiz Abū Ṭāhir Zubāir 'Alī Za'ī]
58) ISBN [9-117-59-9960-978]; Edition [2nd]; Published [1429H]; Vol [1]; Researcher [Shaykh Muḥammad Nāṣiruddīn Al-Albānī]
59) Titled by Dārussalām as Jāmi' At-Tirmidhī
60) Published [1430H]; Vol [1]; Researcher [Ḥāfiz Abū Ṭāhir Zubāir 'Alī Za'ī]
61) ISBN [0-123-59-9960-978]; Edition [2nd]; Published [1429H]; Vol [1]; Researcher [Shaykh Muḥammad Nāṣiruddīn Al-Albānī]
62) Published [1430H]; Vol [1]; Researcher [Ḥāfiz Abū Ṭāhir Zubāir 'Alī Za'ī]
63) ISBN [3-122-59-9960-978]; Edition [2nd]; Published [1429H]; Vol [1]; Researcher [Shaykh Muḥammad Nāṣiruddīn Al-Albānī]
64) ISBN [2-7451-0945-6]; Edition [2nd]; Published [1433H]; Vol [2]; Researcher [Shaykh Muḥammad 'Abdul-Azīz Al-Khālidī]
65) ISBN [978-9933-446-46-8]; Edition [1st]; Published [1438H]; Vol [1]; Researcher [Kulāl Ḥasan 'Alī]; Version [Yaḥyā Bin Yaḥyā]
66) Edition [1st]; Published [1416H]; Vol [50]; Researcher [Shaykh Shu'ayb Al-Arnā'ūt]
67) Edition [2nd]; Published [1422H]; Vol [1]; Researcher [Shaykh Shu'ayb Al-Arnā'ūt]
68) Edition [1st]; Published [1424H]; Vol [6]; Researcher [Shaykh Shu'ayb Al-Arnā'ūt]
69) ISBN [2-7451-0948-0]; Edition [2nd]; Published [1424H]; Vol [11]; Researcher [Muḥammad 'Abdul-Qādir 'Aṭā]
70) Edition [1st]; Published [1411H]; Vol [2]

Printed in Great Britain
by Amazon

57689268R00028